Using Basic English Gra

FORM AND FUNCTION

OTHER TITLES OF INTEREST INCLUDE:

Using English Grammar, *E. Woods and N. McLeod*
Using Idioms, *J. B. Heaton and T. W. Noble*
Using Phrasal Verbs, *D. Britten and G. Dellar*
International Expressways, *S. Molinsky and B. Bliss*

Using Basic English Grammar
FORM AND FUNCTION

Edward G. Woods
The Institute for English Language Education
LANCASTER UNIVERSITY

Nicole J. McLeod
The Institute for English Language Education
LANCASTER UNIVERSITY

INCLUDES ANSWER KEY

Prentice Hall

New York   London   Toronto   Sydney   Tokyo   Singapore

PRENTICE HALL INTERNATIONAL ENGLISH LANGUAGE TEACHING

First published 1992 by
Prentice Hall International (UK) Ltd
Campus 400, Maylands Avenue
Hemel Hempstead
Hertfordshire, HP2 7EZ
A division of
Simon & Schuster International Group

Designed by Caroline Archer
Illustrations by Pat Drennan

Typeset in 9/11 pt Palatino
by Fakenham Photosetting Ltd, Fakenham, Norfolk

Printed and bound in Great Britain
by Dotesios Ltd, Trowbridge, Wiltshire

Library of Congress Cataloging-in-Publication Data

Woods, Edward G., 1937–
    Using basic English grammar: form and function / Edward Woods &
Nicole McLeod.
      p.   cm. – (Prentice Hall English language teaching)
    Includes index.
    ISBN 0–13–952656–0: $11.95
    1. English language – Grammar – Study and teaching.   I. McLeod,
Nicole J. 1936–   .   II. Title.   III. Series.
PE1065.W66   1992
428.2 – dc20
                                                                      92–749
                                                                      CIP

British Library Cataloguing in Publication Data

A catalogue record for this book is available from
the British Library

ISBN 0–13–952656–0

1 2 3 4 5   96   95   94   93   92

CONTENTS

SECTION 3
DETERMINERS

SECTION 4
MODIFICATION

SECTION 5

CONNECTING

APPENDICES

INDEX

ANSWER KEY

ACKNOWLEDGEMENTS

Our thanks to all those who encouraged us to write this follow-up to USING ENGLISH GRAMMAR – MEANING AND FORM, especially David Haines and our editor Isobel Fletcher de Téllez.

We should also like to thank Dr Antoine Vermeire and Herr Konrad Lange who read the manuscript and made very useful and perceptive comments.

And also, once again, our thanks to Pat Drennan for her illustrations, and Julia Dall and Valerie Mendes for their work in the production of the book.

The publishers and the authors acknowledge with thanks permission from 'The Guardian' to reproduce copyright material on pages 188 and 191.

EDWARD WOODS and NICOLE MCLEOD

INTRODUCTION

1. TO THE TEACHER

This book should be used as a reference and a source of simple explanations and interesting tasks for your learners. If they are beginners, then it would probably be useful to translate some parts of the explanations into their mother tongue if they all speak the same first language. Although the use of the mother tongue can be very helpful to the understanding of the grammatical concepts, the learners should be encouraged to use English in all the tasks and the tasks themselves should be done in pairs or small groups. In the units some language for classroom interaction is included so that the learners can negotiate in English while setting up the task. For example, they will learn such expressions as:

It's your turn now.

Shall I help you?

You should also encourage them to use other language of negotiation and interaction such as:

I'll start.

Let's try the second task.

We need a secretary to take notes. Who wants to do it?

The learners should be encouraged to look for cognates – words that have similar sounds and meanings in their own language or languages – and to spot 'false friends' – words that have similar sounds or spellings but that mean something quite different in their own languages as, for example, *simpático* and *sympathetic*, which do not mean the same in Spanish/Portuguese and English.

The learners should also be encouraged to look for similarities and differences between English and their own languages in the structures of the languages. In other words, they should be encouraged to draw on all their knowledge in learning English and not view the English class as something remote from reality or the English language as something totally foreign and unrelated to their own languages.

You should go over the section **'To the learner'** with your learners so that they understand what the book aims to do. You may find that it will help if you translate this section.

2. TO THE LEARNER

This book will help you to learn how to use English right from the beginning. It will teach you the grammar of English and will also teach you how and when you can use each grammatical form that you learn. You will also learn some common and useful expressions and some of the language you will need to know to do the tasks in English.

If you are working on your own with this book you will find the answers to most of the tasks in the back. But learning a language means learning to use a language and to communicate with others in that language. So it will be most helpful to you if you can find a friend or colleague to work with so that you can get the most out of the book. Some of the tasks do not have answers because they are for you to practise using English in a free situation and there are many possible answers. Even if you do not have a teacher, you should try these tasks and then try to find out from other people or from reference books whether your answers are correct.

SECTION 1
Words in sentences

Unit 1.1
WORD ORDER:
STATEMENTS
Form

Jamie left.
I saw the news on TV.
Maggie gave John the job.
Pauline Skinner is a composer and writer.

HOW TO FORM THEM

In this section we are talking about what makes a sentence complete grammatically.

Every sentence must have a *verb* and a *subject*. The subject comes before the verb.

What happens after the verb depends on the type of verb. What we call the *transitivity* of the verb.

With some verbs, the sentence is complete when there is just a subject and verb. These are called *intransitive* verbs.

With other verbs, the sentence isn't grammatically complete unless something comes afterwards. These are *transitive* verbs.

The verb is very important in the sentence.

Intransitive verbs

These are verbs, where it is only necessary to have the subject and verb:

> Jamie left.

In this sentence, *Jamie* is the subject and *left* is the verb:

> SUBJECT + VERB (S + V)

The subject answers the question *who?* or *what?* before the verb:

> Who left?
> Jamie left.

2

Grammatically this is an acceptable sentence and it is not necessary for anything to follow the verb. We can, of course, add other information:

Jamie left <u>at 8 o'clock.</u>
S + V + (Adv.)

The phrase underlined (an adverbial phrase) gives us more information, but without it the sentence would still be grammatically correct.

Transitive verbs

These are verbs where there must be something after the verb.

(i) with a direct object only:
I saw the news on television.

Saw is a verb that needs to have something after it. In this example we have *the news*. This is called the *direct object*. It answers the question *who?* or *what?* after the verb:

What did you see?
I saw the news.

Once again, the sentence is grammatically correct without the adverbial phrase.

3

WARNING BOX

There are some transitive verbs where the adverbial is necessary to make the sentence correct grammatically. For example, we cannot say:

    * The mother put the meat.

That is not a complete statement. We must add an adverbial:

    The mother put the meat *on the table.*

    S + V + Odir + Adv.

With verbs like *put,* we must be told **where** something was put and so an adverbial must be included.

Here is another example:

    She treated him *badly.*

In this example we must be told **how** the person was treated and so the adverb is essential.

(ii) with an indirect object:

    Maggie gave John the job.

Other verbs also need an indirect object. In this example, the answer to the question *who?* or *what?* after the verb is *the job. John* answers the question *to whom?*:

    Maggie gave John the job.
    S + V + Oind + Odir

We can rephrase the statement as:

    Maggie gave the job to John.
    S + V + Odir + Oind

NOTE: Some other verbs which take an indirect object are *send, write, read, teach.*

4

Intensive verbs

These are also *transitive* verbs, but in some cases, what comes after the verb is a description of the subject:

>Pauline Skinner is a composer and writer.

A composer and writer tells us more about Pauline Skinner. So in this example, what comes after the verb is called a *complement*:

>Pauline Skinner is a composer and writer.
>S + V + C

NOTE: Some other verbs which are followed by a complement are *become, seem, feel*.

SUMMARY

Subject S	Verb V	Complement C	Direct object Odir	Indirect object Oind	Adverbial Adv.
Jamie	left				at 8.00
I	saw		the news		on TV
Maggie	gave		the job	John	
Pauline Skinner	is	a composer and writer			

TASK ONE

Complete the following table by putting the words from the sentences in the right column.

	Subject	Verb	Complement	Direct object	Indirect object	Adverbial
(a)						
(b)						
(c)						
(d)						
(e)						
(f)						
(g)						
(h)						
(i)						
(j)						

(a) He woke up early.
(b) Edward Young wrote novels.
(c) The Queen gave the captain a medal.
(d) Elizabeth became Queen in 1952.
(e) She seemed very ill that day.
(f) The light went out.
(g) The dog bit the postman.
(h) Mr Blandings builds his dream house.
(i) Romeo loved Juliet.
(j) Doug taught Andrea English.

6

TASK TWO

Put the following words in the correct order to make sentences.
(a)   next is she week coming
(b)   prize boy a the won
(c)   kiss him gave a she
(d)   young the blushed boy
(e)   ill man was the
(f)   easily tired he became
(g)   father girl disobeyed her the
(h)   walking she dustman the with was
(i)   Diane him the gave money beer the for
(j)   liked her he

```
┌─────────────────────────────────────────┐
│                                           │
│              Unit 1.2                      │
│           WORD ORDER:                      │
│           QUESTIONS                        │
│              Form                          │
│                                           │
└─────────────────────────────────────────┘
```

Who came to the meeting?
What's his name?
Where did she go?
When are you going to Madrid?
Why did you say that?
How will I know?

Who? What? Where? When? Why? How?

HOW TO USE THEM

Who, What, Where, When, Why and *How* are question words. They are used to form questions and often come at the beginning.

Who and *What* can be used as subjects as well as question words. If they are used this way, the order for the question is:

Subject (Who/What)	Verb	Object	Example
Who	is	that man	Who is that man over there?
What	is	your name	What is your name?
Who	was playing	the piano	Who was playing the piano this morning?
What	happened		What happened last night?
Who	is coming		Who is coming to dinner?
Who	came		Who came to the meeting?

When we use *Who, What, When, Where, Why* or *How* as question words, the form of the question is very regular. The order of other words after these question words is the same as the order of questions. (See the Units in Section 2 to find out how questions are formed.)

8

Question word	Verb	Subject	Verb	Example
Who	are	you	going to	Who are you going to meet tomorrow?
Who	did	you	meet	Who did you meet yesterday?
What	is	she	studying	What is she studying at college?
What	did	he	say	What did he say to her?
Where	are	they	going	Where are they going for their holidays?
Where	will	you	go	Where will you go after school?
When	did	we	see	When did we last see you?
Why	did	you	say	Why did you say that?
How	will	I	know	How will I know the answer is right?

TASK ONE

*Put **Who, What, When, Where, Why** or **How** in the blanks in these sentences*

(a) .... did they invite to the party?
(b) .... are you looking so sad?
(c) .... are you going for your holidays?
(d) .... isn't he going to the meeting?
(e) .... does it work?
(f) .... is my pencil?
(g) .... won the 1990 World Cup?
(h) .... did she say to you?
(i) .... does she know the answer?
(j) .... do you think you will have finished?

TASK TWO

*Make questions using **Who, What, When, Where, Why** or **How** with the following verbs. Try to use each of the question words at least once and to use different verb forms.*

For example:
　　run
　　Why are you running?
　　Who ran out of the house?

(a) buy
(b) get
(c) sit
(d) go
(e) bring
(f) find
(g) read
(h) jump
(i) ask
(j) live

10

```
┌─────────────────────────────────────┐
│                                     │
│          Unit 1.3                   │
│       WORD ORDER:                   │
│       QUESTIONS                     │
│          Function                   │
│                                     │
└─────────────────────────────────────┘
```

Why is he worried?
How do you do this?
When are we going?

Who? What? Where? When? Why? How?

WHEN TO USE THEM

Who refers to a person:
   Who is coming to dinner?
   Who is that in the green shirt?

What refers to a thing:
   What is that?
   What is your daughter's name?

Where refers to a place:
   Where are you going?
   Where is the theatre?

When refers to a time:
   When are they arriving?
   When did they live in Manila?

Why asks for a reason for something:
   Why did you say that?
   Why is he shouting?

How refers to the way or manner in which something is done:
   How are computers made?
   How did you come to work?

We can also add words to *How*, such as *How long? How far? How much? How many?*:
   How long is the rope?
   How far is Lancaster from London?
   How much does it cost?
   How many books did you buy?

WARNING BOX

These question words are often not stressed in speech, so it is important to listen carefully to be sure whether the person asking the question wants to know, for example, *when* or *where* you are going. If you are not sure what the question is, you can say:

Did you say *when* or *where*?

COMMON EXPRESSIONS

What do you do (for a living)?

What is your job or occupation?

What is it?

This means 'What do you want?' It is often not very polite so you need to be careful when you use it.

What about . . . ?

This is a way of making a suggestion. It is always followed by the *-ing* form.

What about going out for dinner?

What can I do for you?

This means 'How can I help you?

Who is it?

If someone rings your doorbell or knocks at your door you can ask them to tell you their name by asking 'Who is it?'

(knock at the door)
A. *Who is it?*
B. It's Philip.
C. Oh. Come in, Philip. What can I do for you?

Who knows?

We use this expression when we want to say 'I don't know.'

A. What's the average cost of a house in Quito?
B. *Who knows?* Why don't you ask Marcia. She lives there.

How come . . . ?	This means 'Why is it that . . . ?

A. How come you're so late?
B. I missed the bus.

How about . . . ?

This is a way of making a suggestion or an offer. It can be followed by a noun or the *-ing* form.

A. I don't know what to do this evening.
B. How about coming to my house for a meal?

Why not . . . ?

This is also used to make a suggestion or an offer.

A. I really can't understand what he says.
B. Why not ask him to speak more slowly?

TASK ONE

*Think of 12 things about yourself that could be the answers to **Who, What, When, Where, Why** or **How** questions so that you have two questions with each question word. Write down the answers on the right side of a piece of paper. Then exchange your paper with a partner and try to write the questions for your partner's answers while your partner writes the questions for your answers. When you have written as many questions as you can, check with your partner.*

For example:

14 July.
Because I want to improve my English.
By bus.

(The questions were: When is your birthday?
Why are you studying English?
How did you come to class today?)

TASK TWO

*Cut a sheet of paper into 16 pieces. Print or type 8 questions using **How long . . . ? How far . . . ? How much . . . ? How many . . . ?** Put one question on each piece of paper.*

Then write the answers to your 8 questions, putting one answer on each piece of paper.

Mix up all the questions and answers that you and your colleagues have written and give out the pieces of paper so that everyone has 16 pieces each.

Make as many pairs of questions and answers with your 16 pieces as you can and then go around to the others and try to find questions or answers to match the ones you have left over.

If there are some questions and answers that don't match at the end, make up new questions or answers that could match them.

TASK THREE

Read the situations below and choose a common expression you could use.

For example:

Your friend says he is feeling very unhappy. What could you say?
You: Why don't you watch a comedy film on television?

(a) You are at a party and meet an interesting person. You want to know more about this person. What could you say?
(b) Your friend comes into your office and says he needs something. What would you say?
(c) Your doorbell rings late at night. You don't want to let a stranger into your house. What do you say?

(d) Your friend calls you from the other room. How can you find out what he or she wants?

(e) You were going to meet your friend at the cinema one evening but he or she didn't arrive. When you meet him/her the next day, what could you say?

(f) Someone asks you, 'When is there going to be an election?' You really don't know. What can you say?

(g) A group of friends are planning an outing. Everyone is making suggestions. You want to go to a new play at the theatre. What can you say to suggest this?

Unit 1.4
WORD ORDER: IMPERATIVE
Form

Stop!
Stop the car!
Close the door!
Don't look back.
Don't think me silly.

HOW TO USE IT

We use the *imperative* form to give orders. In unit 1.1, you saw the usual sentence pattern:

Peter stopped the car immediately.
S + V + O + Adv.

When we give orders, we are always talking to the person directly, so the subject is left out:

 Stop!
 V

So, the forms for the imperative can be:
 Stop (the car immediately)!
 V(+ O + Adv.)
Or
 Stop (the car)!
 V(+ O)
Or
 Stop (immediately)!
 V (+ Adv.)
Or
 Stop!
 V

Note that only the verb is essential.

Positive and negative

The examples above use the positive form of the verb *stop*. To form the negative, we put *don't* before the verb:

 Don't stop!
 Don't stop the car!
 Don't look back!
 Don't think me silly.

TASK ONE

Work round the circle below as often as you like and see how many correctly formed imperatives you can find. You must keep the words in the order you find them. You can start at any point in the circle.

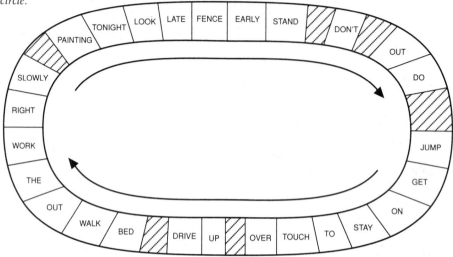

TASK TWO

Now fit the imperatives you have found in TASK ONE with the pictures below.

Unit 1.5
WORD ORDER: IMPERATIVE
Function

Teach English in Japan.
Sell too cheaply and you'll go bankrupt.
Don't touch! This sculpture is very fragile.
In case of emergency, pull the cord.

WHEN TO USE IT

We use the *imperative* form:

(a) to give orders:
Stop!
Come back!
Don't go!

(b) to give instructions:
Then add the tomatoes.
Press the lever down gently.

(c) to give advice:
In case of emergency, pull the cord.
Sell too cheaply and you'll go bankrupt.

(d) to warn someone:
Don't touch! This sculpture is very fragile.
Don't pull out! There's a car.

NOTE: For advice and warning, it is possible to use the conditional form (see Unit 2.35). But we often use the imperative when we must be quick, because it is more direct.

(e) to make a request:
   Please send your CV.
   Please write giving full details.

(f) to invite someone:
   Come to my party next Saturday.

(g) in advertisements, telegrams etc. when there is very little space:
   Teach English in Japan.
   Meet me at airport, 6 o'clock.

COMMON EXPRESSIONS

Don't beat about the bush.	Say exactly what you want to say.
Come down to earth.	Be practical. Don't dream about impossible things.
Don't let the grass grow under your feet.	Do things immediately. Don't waste time.
Get cracking.	Start working immediately.
Put your foot down.	Insist on what you want.

TASK ONE

Identify the functions of the imperative forms used in the short dialogues below:

(a) A: How do I make this?
   B: First, cut the meat into small pieces.

(b) A: What else do you need?
   B: Please send us the application forms as soon as possible.

(c) A: (on the phone) Is that Jean? Are you free tonight?
   B: Yes.
   A: Join us for dinner at the Elliott restaurant.
   B: I'd love to.

(d) A: Why can't we go now?
   B: Get there too early and you'll have to wait outside in the cold.

(e) A: Can I feed the chimpanzees?
   B: All right. But don't go too close!

TASK TWO

When you are reading or listening to English, make a note of the imperative forms used and identify what function they have.

TASK THREE

What would you say to someone in the following situations?

(a) Your friend is complaining that it is important for her to decide on her holiday, but her husband won't make a decision.
(b) You are upset because your friend has had a good idea, but he won't start working on it.
(c) Your colleague makes a good suggestion about a work project, but it will be very expensive and it will take a long time.

21

The war will soon be over.
Charles Dickens never forgot his poor childhood.
The postman always rings twice.

HOW TO USE THEM

Adverbs of frequency always come before the main verb in the sentence:

Charles Dickens *never* forgot his poor childhood.
S + Adv. + V + Odir

This also happens in the following examples where there is another verb as well as the main verb:

I've *never* seen him before.
You must *always* be polite to her.
Cats don't *always* fight dogs?
S + Aux. + Adv. + V + . . .

WARNING BOX

There is one exception and that is the verb to *be*. When *be* is in the present simple (see Unit 2.1) or the past simple (see Unit 2.3), the adverb comes after *be*:

He was *always* late.
She is *often* early.
S + BE + Adv. + . . .

WHEN TO USE THEM

Adverbs like *always*, *never*, *sometimes*, *often*, tell you **how often** something happens or happened:

The postman *always* rings twice.

Always here tells you how often the postman rings.

Adverbs like *soon, already,* tell you **when** something happens or happened:

The war will *soon* be over.

Soon here tells you when the war will be over.

These adverbs are used to answer the following questions:

(i) how often:
    A.   How often can you see Mt Fuji from Tokyo?
    B.   You can *never* see Mt Fuji from Tokyo. There is too much pollution.

(ii) when:
    A.   When will the TV play begin?
    B.   It has *already* begun.

(iii) questions which have *ever* in them:
    Have you ever been to Genoa?
    Do you ever go climbing?

    When the answers to these questions is 'Yes', you do not use *ever* in the answer:
    A.   Have you ever been to Genoa?
    B.   Yes, I've *often* been to Genoa.

    When the answer is 'No', you can use *ever*, but you usually use *never*:
    A.   Do you ever go climbing?
    B.   No, I *never* go climbing.
      * *No, I don't ever go climbing* is not often used.

The relationship between the adverbs which answer the question **how often** can be shown like this:

always... (100%)
usually ....
often ....
sometimes..(50%)
seldom ....
rarely ....
never (0%)

TASK ONE

Put one of these adverbs into the sentences beneath.

soon   already   often   seldom   always   sometimes   never   rarely   usually   ever

(a) John will be here.
(b) Do you go to Italy for your holidays?
(c) Charles Dickens forgot his poor childhood.
(d) The milkman calls on Monday for his money.
(e) I've seen that film.
(f) I will remember you.
(g) Lions attack people first.
(h) The prince had dinner with his wife.
(i) Europe will be united.
(j) Have you tried to swim across the channel?

TASK TWO

Exchange your answers to TASK ONE with a friend and see if you agree on the choice of the adverb used.

If you don't agree, see what the difference in meaning is.

SECTION 2
Verbs

The population of Bahrain is 400 000.
Bacteria are everywhere.
Hamburg is the greenest city in Germany.
Most modern bicycles have gears.

HOW TO FORM THE AFFIRMATIVE

The two most common irregular verbs are *be* and *have*. The **subject** and the form of the verb *be* are often joined. In speech, *am, are* and *is* are usually shortened [or contracted] to *'m, 're* or *'s*:

Subject	Be		Example	
I	am	['m]	I am hungry.	I'm hungry.
You	are	['re]	You are intelligent.	You're intelligent.
He	is	['s]	He is old.	He's old.
She	is	['s]	She is amusing.	She's amusing.
It	is	['s]	It is expensive.	It's expensive.
We	are	['re]	We are late.	We're late.
They	are	['re]	They are early.	They're early.

Subject	Have	Example	
I You We They	have ['ve got]	I have a blue car. You have nice eyes. We have a new textbook. They have lots of money.	I've got a blue car. You've got nice eyes. We've got a new textbook. They've got lots of money.
She He It	has ['s got]	She has a computer. He has a red car. It has an index.	She's got a computer He's got a red car. It's got an index.

In speech, *have* is usually shortened [contracted] to *'ve* and joined to the subject, and *has* is usually shortened to *'s*. This is especially true in British English. When British people make the contraction with *'ve* or *'s*, we usually add *got*:

I*'ve got* a blue car.
She*'s got* a computer.

This is less common in ·American English where the contractions *'ve* and *'s* are less common:

I *have* a blue car.
She *has* a computer.

They are not used in more formal written English whether British or American.

27

HOW TO FORM THE NEGATIVE

BE

To form negative sentences with *be* add *not* after the form of the verb *be*. There are two ways of shortening [contracting] the forms. You can either shorten *not* to *n't* and add it to the form of the verb *be*:

He *isn't* interested.

Or shorten the form of the verb *be* and add it to the noun or pronoun subject:

He's *not* interested.

If you do this, the *not* stands out and the sentence can sound more emphatic.

With *I* you can only shorten *am* to *'m* and add it to *I*:

I'm *not* interested.

Subject	Be	not	Example	
I	am	not		I'm not very happy.
She			She isn't thirsty.	She's not thirsty.
He	is	not [isn't]	He isn't stupid.	He's not stupid.
It			It isn't useful.	It's not useful.
You			You aren't ready.	You're not ready.
We	are	not [aren't]	We aren't hungry.	We're not hungry.
They			They aren't bored.	They're not bored.

$$-x^2 - 5x + 4$$
$$10x^2 - 121x$$
$$10x-1)(x-12)$$
$$=$$

HAVE

With *have* it depends on whether you add *got* or not. If you add *got* then you add *not* to the form of the verb *have*:

Subject	Have/Has	not	Got	Example
I You We They	have	not [haven't]	got	I haven't got a bicycle. You haven't got a book. We haven't got time. They haven't got a car.
She He It	has	not [hasn't]	got	She hasn't got a pencil. He hasn't got a pen. It hasn't got a heater.

If you don't add *got*, you usually use a form of the verb *do* plus *not* before the verb *have*:

Subject	Do/Does	not		Have	Example
I You We They	do	not	[don't]	have	I don't have a bicycle. You don't have a book. We don't have time. They don't have a car.
She He It	does	not	[doesn't]	have	She doesn't have a pencil. He doesn't have a pen. It doesn't have a heater.

If you don't use *got*, you can put *not* after the form of the verb *have*. With this negative form, we always shorten *not* to *n't* and join it to the form of the verb *has*:

We *haven't* time.

He *hasn't* any brothers.

HOW TO FORM QUESTIONS

BE

Put the form of the verb *be* in front of the subject to make a question:

Be	Subject	Example
am	I	Am I late?
are	you we they	Are you tired? Are we on time? Are they here?
is	she he it	Is she hungry? Is he tall? Is it green?

The answer can be 'Yes' or 'No' but we usually add the pronoun and the form of the verb *be* to the answer:

    Am I late?   Yes, *you are.*
    Are they here?   No, *they are*n't.

31

HAVE

When you add *got* to *have*, form the question by putting *have* or *has* in front of the subject and *got* after the subject:

Have/Has	Subject	Got	Example
Have	I you we they	got	Have I got enough time? Have you got a car? Have we got enough money? Have they got any books?
Has	she he it	got	Has she got a pen? Has he got a pencil? Has it got any disadvantages?

The answer can be 'Yes' or 'No' but we usually add the pronoun and the form of the verb *have* to the answer:

Have you got a car?　　　　Yes, *I have.*
Have they got any books?　No, *they haven't.*

WARNING BOX

If you add *got* to the answer, then you have to add something like 'one' or another number or a quantity determiner like 'many' or 'a lot'.

Has it got any disadvantages?　　Yes it has.
　　　　　　　　　　　　　　　　Yes, *it's got many.*
　　　　　　　　　　　　　　　　No, it hasn't.
　　　　　　　　　　　　　　　　No, it *hasn't got any.*
Have you got a car?　　　　　　No, I *haven't got one.*
　　　　　　　　　　　　　　　　Yes, *I've got one.*

If you use *have* without *got*, then the questions can be formed in one of two ways.

The first way is to treat the verb *have* as a normal regular verb and put a form of the verb *do* in front of the subject:

Do/Does	Subject	Have	Example
Do	I you we they	have	Do I have enough time? Do you have a car? Do we have enough money? Do they have any books?
Does	she he it	have	Does she have a pen? Does he have a pencil? Does it have any disadvantages?

The answer can be 'Yes' or 'No' but we usually add the pronoun and the form of the verb *do* to the answer:

Do you have a car?	Yes, *I do*. No, *I don't*.
Do we have enough money?	Yes, we *do*. No, *we don't*.

The second way is to put the form of the verb *have* in front of the subject:

Have I enough time?
Have they any books?
Has it any disadvantages?

This is a less common form of question with *have*. The answer can be 'Yes' or 'No' but we usually add the pronoun and the form of the verb *have* to the answer:

Have they any books?	Yes, *they have.*
	No, *they haven't.*
Has it any disadvantages?	Yes, *it has.*
	No, *it hasn't.*

WARNING BOX

Be careful how you use the answer 'Of course' when you are answering questions. If it is a question asking for information, do not say 'Of course' as this can sound very rude. It suggests that the person has asked a stupid question. 'Of course' should be used when someone has asked you to do something or made a request in the form of a question.

Can you help me?	Yes, of course.
Do you mind closing the window?	No, of course not.

These are requests so it is right to say 'Of course'.

Can you swim?	No, I can't.
Are you married?	Yes, I am.

These are questions asking for information so you cannot say 'Of course'.

TASK ONE

*Fill in a form of the verb **be** or a form of the verb **have** in the blanks in the following passages.*

(a) Swans .... large birds – almost 4 feet tall. They .... long necks. Some swans .... very tame. They often come near people for food. Females usually .... about six babies which are called cygnets. Cygnets .... grey in colour and .... very small wings but when they are fully grown they .... large and strong wings and .... white in colour. Swans can live to be 40.

(b) Jean de Brunhoff wrote the first Babar book for children in 1931. Babar .... the name of the hero. He .... an elephant. He .... a friend called Zephir who .... a monkey. He also .... a cousin called Arthur and a wife called Celeste. Babar .... polite, friendly and reliable. He and the other elephants .... many adventures in the jungle and in the city called Celesteville. The Babar books have been translated from French into many languages. There .... now a cartoon series which is shown all over the world.

(c) Water .... the most important compound on Earth. It can exist in three states – vapour, liquid and solid (ice). About $2\frac{1}{2}$ per cent of the Earth's water .... in glaciers. Most of the rest .... liquid.

(d) Electricity .... the most useful form of energy. It .... easy to produce; it .... easy to transmit over long distances; it .... clean and .... no smell. Above all it .... very convenient.

35

TASK TWO

*Fill in the blanks in the following passages with **is/are** or **has/have**. This is a written text so you should not use **has got/have got**.*

Nuts .... a dried fruit in a shell and .... full of goodness – protein and vitamins. They .... a high fibre content. Almonds .... a high calcium content. They .... also full of protein. They .... many uses in cooking and can also be eaten raw. Brazil nuts .... full of zinc, protein and vitamin B1. They .... very hard shells. Cashews .... not nuts. They .... legumes, like peanuts. They .... a delicate flavour and .... delicious cooked with fish and rice dishes. Peanuts .... the best known and most widely eaten nuts in the world but they .... not actually nuts at all. They .... very high in protein and .... the eight essential amino acids. Peanuts .... also high in calories.

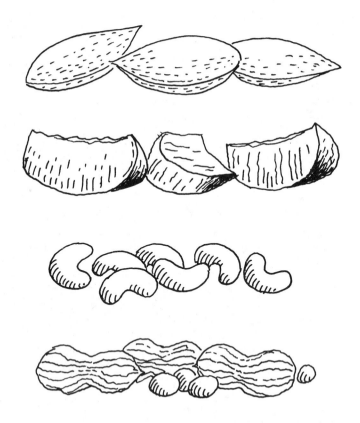

36

Unit 2.2
BE, HAVE:
PRESENT SIMPLE
Function

The baby's hungry.
They have six children.
Have you got any pets?

WHEN TO USE THEM

BE

We use forms of the verb *be*:

(a) to express our feelings:
   I'*m* bored.
   She'*s* happy.
   They'*re* sad.

(b) to express physical feelings:
    The baby's hungry.
    He's thirsty.
    I'm tired.

(c) to give our occupations or professions:
    I'm a teacher trainer.
    She's his accountant.
    She's the personnel manager for the university.
    He's a lecturer.
    They're builders.

NOTE: With these forms we use *a* or *an* or another determiner with singular nouns.

(d) to talk about people's appearances, characteristics or personalities:
    They're intelligent students.
    He's a helpful man.
    She's a young woman.

NOTE: With these forms we use *a* or *an* or another determiner with singular nouns.

(e) to apologise:
   I'*m* sorry.
   I'*m* very sorry I can't come to your party.

(f) to introduce ourselves and others:
   I'*m* Nicki and this is Edward.
   I'*m* Joan and I work at the Institute for English Language Education at Lancaster
   University.

(g) to describe the weather:
   It'*s* raining.
   It'*s* very hot/cold/windy today.

(h) to describe situations:
   It'*s* a difficult problem.
   It'*s* an interesting idea.

(i) to talk about the time:
   What time *is* it?
   It'*s* time to go.
   It'*s* 3 o'clock.

(j) to describe places:
   Grasmere *is* in the Lake District.
   It'*s* a hilly area.
   Hamburg *is* the greenest city in Germany.
   Lancaster *is* in the north-west of England.

HAVE

We use *have* or *have got*:

(a) to show possession or talk about the things we own:
  I *have* (I've *got*) a blue car.
  He's *got* a new pair of shoes.
  They've *got* new books.

NOTE: With these forms we use *a* or *an* or another determiner with singular nouns.

(b) to say how many people there are in our family:
  They've *got* one daughter.
  She's *got* a sister and two brothers.
  They *have* six children.

NOTE: With these forms we use *a* or *an* or another determiner with singular nouns.

(c) to talk about illnesses or health conditions:
  I *have* a headache.

In British English *a* is not usually used with the following conditions but it is used in American English:

British English	American English
I*'ve got* ear ache.	I *have* an ear ache.
I*'ve got* toothache.	I *have* a toothache.
I*'ve got* backache.	I *have* a backache.

With conditions like flu, diabetes, angina and high blood pressure, we do not use *a* or *an*:

He*'s got* flu.

She*'s got* high blood pressure.

(d) to talk about time:

Have you *got* the time?

I *haven't got* enough time to finish this project.

WARNING BOX

If you use 'There . . .' to start the sentence in the present simple, then use *is*, not *have*:

There isn't enough time to finish the project.

We've got plenty of time to finish this report.

(e) to describe the contents of a place:

The house *has* six bedrooms.

They*'ve got* 50 000 books in the library.

It*'s got* 50 000 books.

NOTE: *It's* can mean *it is* or *it has*.

(f) to talk about ideas or problems:

I*'ve got* an idea. Why don't we try it this way?

They*'ve got* many problems.

NOTE: We use *a* or *an* or another determiner in this form if the noun is singular and countable.

(g) to describe people's appearance of personality:

She*'s got* a kind face.

The teacher*'s got* a lot of patience.

He*'s got* small feet.

NOTE: We use *a* or *an* or another determiner in this form if the noun is singular and countable.

41

COMMON EXPRESSIONS

BE

How are you?

This means 'How are you feeling?' But it is often used as part of a greeting, especially in American English. The reply is something like 'Fine', or 'Okay' and you do not talk about your health.

A.   Hi. *How are you?*
B.   I'm fine. *How are you?*

What's up?

This means 'What's happening?'

A.   'Everyone is running out of the building. *What's up?*
B.   There's a fire in the office!

HAVE

Have a go at it.

This means 'Try to do it'.

A.   This is very difficult.
B.   Well, *have a go at it.* I'll help you.

He/she has a lot on his/her mind.

This means he/she is worried about a lot of things or has a lot of things to think about and plan.

A.   He's looking very angry.
B.   He's not angry. *He has a lot on his mind.*

TASK ONE

*For each of the pictures write a sentence or a question with a form of the verbs **be** or **have**.*

(a)

(b)

(c)

TASK TWO

Find out about one or two of the other learners in your class by asking them questions about their families, things they own, etc.

Then choose one person and write a description. If there is room on the walls, you could write these descriptions on large sheets of paper and put them on the wall for everyone to read.

For example:
Questions:
    Have you got any brothers and sisters (or children);
    Have you got any pets?
    Have you got a house, car, bicycle, etc.
Description:
    Amy has long dark hair and dark eyes. She's got two sisters and a brother. She has
    one daughter. She hasn't got any pets. She has a small house and a green car.

43

Unit 2.3
BE, HAVE:
PAST SIMPLE
Form

Margaret Grace Bondfield was the first British woman cabinet minister.
King Henry VIII had six wives.
The Incas did not have a written language.

The two most common irregular verbs are *be* and *have*.

HOW TO FORM THE AFFIRMATIVE

BE *was* or *were*

Subject	Was/Were	Example
I She He It You We They	was were	I was late to work yesterday. She was early. He was a very happy baby. It was a new idea. You were very angry. We were very busy. They were in the kitchen.

HAVE *had*

Subject	Had	Example
I You She He It We They	had	I had lunch at 12 o'clock You had a long meeting. She had two bicycles. He had an English grandmother. It had a powerful engine. We had lots of time. They had ten children.

HOW TO FORM THE NEGATIVE

BE *was not* or *were not*

To form negative sentences with *be*, add *not* after the form of the verb *be*. The form of the verb *be* and *not* are often joined (*wasn't, weren't*) in speech but not in writing unless it is in very informal notes or letters to friends:

Subject	Was/Were	not	Example	
I			I was not here yesterday.	I wasn't here yesterday.
She			She was not well.	She wasn't well.
He	was	not [wasn't]	He was not very happy.	He wasn't happy.
It			It was not interesting.	It wasn't interesting.
You			You were not ready.	You weren't ready.
We	were	not [weren't]	We were not at the party.	We weren't at the party.
They			They were not in the kitchen.	They weren't in the kitchen.

HAVE *did not have*

With *have* the regular form of the negative is used. This is the same as verbs like *work, play, do* and *go*. *Did* and *not* are often joined (*didn't*) in speech but not in writing unless it is in very informal notes or letters to friends:

Subject	Did	not	Have	Example	
I				I did not have any money.	I didn't have any money.
You				You did not have a book.	You didn't have a book.
She				She did not have her pen.	She didn't have her pen.
He	did	not [didn't]	have	He did not have a car.	He didn't have a car.
It				It did not have an index.	It didn't have an index.
We				We did not have enough time.	We didn't have enough time.
They				They did not have any money.	They didn't have any money.

HOW TO FORM QUESTIONS

BE *was/were*

To make questions, put the form of the verb *be* in front of the subject:

Was/Were	Subject	Example
Was	I	Was I successful?
	she	Was she early for the meeting?
	he	Was he here yesterday?
	it	Was it fun?
	we	Were we successful?
Were	you	Were you late for the appointment?
	they	Were they at home when you phoned?

The answer can be either 'Yes' or 'No' but we usually add the pronoun and the form of the verb *be* to the answer:

Was I successful?   No, *you weren't.*
Was the party fun?   Yes, *it was.*
Were you late?   No, *I wasn't.*

If we don't know the answer we can say 'I don't know'. If we use 'I don't know', we do not usually add the pronoun and *was* or *were*:

Was he here yesterday?   I don't know.

HAVE *had*

With *have* the regular question form is used. This is the same as verbs like *work, play, do* and *go*:

Did	Subject	Have	Example
Did	I you she he we they	have	Did I have a meeting last Monday? Did you go to the cinema with them? Did she buy the book? Did he do the work? Did we have fish for lunch last week? Did they have a holiday last summer?

The answer can be either 'Yes' or 'No' but we usually add the pronoun and *did*:

Did she buy the book?   No, *she didn't*.
Did he do the work?   Yes, *he did*.
Did we have fish for lunch?   Yes, *you* (or *we*) *did*.

If we don't know the answer we can say 'I don't know' and we do not usually use the pronoun and *did*:

Did they have a holiday last summer?   I don't know.

TASK ONE

*Fill in the past form of the verbs 'be' (**was/were**) or 'have' (**had**) in the blanks in the passage below.*

The Bella Coola Indians on the west coast of North America believed the 'HaoHao' .... an enormous man-eating bird. The Indians .... very frightened of the bird. According to legend, it .... huge wings. It also .... a long black beak. The Indians made masks for dancers to wear. The masks .... more than a metre long and the dancer could make the beak move by pulling a string.

TASK TWO

*Fill in the blanks in the following passage with **was/were** or **had**.*

Henry VIII became King of England on 22 April 1509. He .... seventeen years old at the time and he .... too young to be king so a King's Council ruled the country. His first wife .... Catherine of Aragon. She .... the daughter of Isabella of Castille and Ferdinand of Aragon. Her first husband .... Arthur, who .... Henry's elder brother. When Prince Arthur died, Catherine married Henry. They .... one daughter, Mary, who was born in 1516.

In 1526 Henry VIII met Anne Boleyn and fell in love with her. She .... the daughter of Sir Thomas who .... an important and powerful man. A strange fact about Anne Boleyn is that she .... six fingers on her right hand. Henry VIII married Anne Boleyn and she .... a daughter, Elizabeth, soon afterwards, who became Queen Elizabeth I. Because Elizabeth .... not a son, Henry divorced Anne and sentenced her to death in 1536. He then married Jane Seymour and in 1537 she .... a son.

49

BE, HAVE:
PAST SIMPLE
Function

The capital of Brazil was Rio de Janeiro until 1960.
Amy Johnson was the first woman to fly solo from England to Australia.
Marie Curie was a French physicist of Polish birth.

WHEN TO USE THEM

BE   *was* or *were*

1. We can use *was* or *were* for many of the same functions as we use the present forms *is* and *are* if we are talking about the past.

   We can use *was/were*:
   (a) to express our feelings in the past:
        I *was* depressed by the news.
        He *was* sad.
        They *were* happy.

   (b) to express physical feelings:
        The baby *was* ill.
        She *was* tired.
        They *were* thirsty.

   (c) to give occupations or professions in the past:
        He *was* a teacher (and now he is the principal).
        She *was* an accountant (and now she is the manager).
        They *were* customs officers.

NOTE: With these forms we use *a* or *an* or another determiner with singular nouns.

   (d) to talk about people's appearances, characteristics or personalities in the past:
        They *were* good students.
        He *was* a very active child.
        She *was* a happy baby.

NOTE: With these forms we use *a* or *an* or another determiner with singular nouns.

(e) to describe the weather:
It *was* raining.
It *was* very hot/cold/windy yesterday.

(f) to describe situations:
It *was* a difficult decision.
It *was* an interesting project.

(g) to talk about the time:
It *was* 10 o'clock when we started the meeting. Now it's 3 o'clock.
They *were* at the beach by 9 o'clock.

2.
(a) We use *was* or *were* to state a fact that was true in the past but that is no longer true:
The Federal District of Rio de Janeiro *was* the capital of Brazil until 1960.

(b) We can also use it to talk about an event or fact in the past:
Amy Johnson *was* the first woman to fly solo from England to Australia.
Marie Curie *was* a French physicist of Polish birth.

HAVE *had*

We can use *had* for many of the same functions as we use the present forms *has* and *had* if we are talking about the past. We do not add *got* for these meanings or functions of *had*.

We can use *had*:
(a) to show possession or talk about the things people owned in the past:
  We *had* a red car in Malaysia.
  He *had* a private plane when he worked in California.

NOTE: With these forms we use *a* or *an* or another determiner with singular nouns.

(b) to say how many people there were in a family:
  President Kennedy *had* two children, a daughter and a son.

NOTE: With these forms we use *a* or *an* or another determiner with singular nouns.

(c) to talk about illnesses or health conditions in the past:
  He *had* flu last week.
  (See Units 3.2, 3.3 and Appendix 3 for when to use *a* or *an*.)

(d) to talk about time in the past:
  I *had* no time to do the report.
  She didn't *have* enough time to finish the work.

WARNING BOX

If you use 'There . . .' to start the sentence, then use *was* in the past simple, not *had*:
There *wasn't* enough time to finish the project.

(e) to describe the contents of a place in the past:
  Their house in Havana *had* four bedrooms.
  Hampton Court Palace *had* four kitchens.

(f) to talk about ideas, problems, etc.:
  The students *had* no problems with the Thai exam.
  We *had* a problem with the car and arrived late.
  The teacher *had* too many pupils in the class.

NOTE: We use *a* or *an* or another determiner in this form if the noun is singular and countable.

(g) to describe people's appearances, personalities or careers in the past:
     She *had* a brilliant career.
     He *had* a long beard.

NOTE: We use *a* or *an* or another determiner in this form if the noun is singular and countable.

TASK ONE

*Choose a famous person in history and write a short biography of that person. Because the person is dead you will be using the past forms of the verbs. Use as many past forms of the verbs **be** and **have** as you can.*

For example:

John F. Kennedy was the 35th President of the United States. He was a Democrat. His wife, Jacqueline, was very popular and very interested in the arts. He had two children, a daughter and a son.

Indira Gandhi was the first woman Prime Minister of India. She was the daughter of Jawaharlal Nehru. She had two sons.

TASK TWO

Join with a partner and discuss your own and her/his past life. What did you feel, think, have, etc. when you were 10 years old? Write down some of the facts and then check with the others in your group so that you can make a poster summarising all the facts about the people in your group.

For example:

Name [age then]	Pets	Belongings	Personality	Illnesses
John [10]	cat	red bicycle	cheerful	malaria
Marcia [10]	parrot	roller skates	quiet	measles

TASK THREE

What changes have taken place in your town or city since you were young? Discuss these changes with a partner and make a list of the town/city then and now.

For example: Rio de Janeiro:

There were streetcars called 'bondes'.   There are no 'bondes' now.
They had lots of fish in the lake.   There are no fish now.
The roads were narrow.   They are wide now.

Unit 2.5
PRESENT SIMPLE
Form

Some vegetarians eat fish.

Mina plays tennis every weekend.

The city of Paris spends £150 million each year on cleaning the streets.

HOW TO FORM IT

For *I, you, we, they* use the simple stem of the verb:

> I *play*
> you *play*
> we *play*
> they *play*

NOTE: Although there is a singular and a plural *you* in English, the form of the verb is always the same for both and so in this book we will only put *you* once in the list.

For *he, she* and *it* add *-s* to the stem:

> he *plays*
> she *plays*
> it *plays*

Sometimes you have to make other changes. If the word ends in a consonant + *y*, change the last letter of the word to *-i* and add *-es:*

> study   becomes *studies*
> cry   becomes *cries*

If the word ends in *-ch* or *-sh* or *-o*, add *-es:*

> watch   becomes *watches*
> finish   becomes *finishes*
> go   becomes *goes*
> do   becomes *does*

55

<table>
<tr><td>

WARNING BOX

One of the things that learners find most difficult to remember is to add the *-s* or *-es* to the verb when they use *he, she* or *it*. So you need to practise this form and try to correct yourself every time you leave off the *-s*.

</td></tr>
</table>

HOW TO FORM THE NEGATIVE

To form negative sentences, add a form of the verb *do* plus *not* before the stem of the verb. These are often joined to form *don't* or *doesn't*:

Subject	Do not	Stem	Example
I		drink	I don't drink tea.
			I do not drink tea.
You		watch	You don't watch sports on television.
	do not [don't]		You do not watch sports on television.
We		sing	We don't sing in the streets.
			We do not sing in the streets.
They		eat	Vegetarians don't eat meat.
			Vegetarians do not eat meat.
She		speak	Katie doesn't speak Spanish.
			Katie does not speak Spanish.
He	does not [doesn't]	play	Jamie doesn't play ice-hockey.
			Jamie does not play ice-hockey.
It		like	My cat doesn't like loud noises.
			My cat does not like loud noises.

NOTE: The *-es* is added to *do* but the stem is not changed.

HOW TO FORM QUESTIONS

Put *do* or *does* before the subject and the verb stem to make a question:

Do	Subject	Stem	Example
Do	I you we they	speak drink leave like	Do I speak clearly? Do you drink coffee for breakfast? Do we leave at 6.30? Do teachers like testing their students?
Does	she he it	know eat rain	Does Katie know any French songs? Does Jamie eat rice? Does it rain a lot in June?

NOTE: The *-es* is added to *do* but the stem is not changed.

The answer can be 'Yes' or 'No' but we usually add the pronoun and a form of the verb *do*:

Do I speak clearly?	Yes, *you do*.
Do you drink coffee for breakfast?	Yes, *I do*.
Do we sing well?	No, *you do*n't.
Do teachers like testing their students?	No, many teachers *do*n't.
Does Katie know any French songs?	Yes, *she does*.
Does Jamie eat rice?	No, *he doesn't*.
Does it rain a lot in June?	No, *it doesn't*.

TASK ONE

Fill in the missing words in the following charts:

I .... You eat He eats She .... It	We eat They	I drink You .... He .... She drinks It	We .... They drink

Now make sentences from your chart by adding words from the following list or by adding words of your own:

    coffee   tea   fish   potatoes   cheese   milk   eggs   water

TASK TWO

Make a chart like the chart in TASK ONE using different verbs. Leave some of the spaces blank and exchange your work with a partner. Then each of you can fill in the other's chart. Finally, check with your partner and another pair to see if you have made any mistakes. Your teacher can help with the final check.

TASK THREE

Fill in the blanks in the following passage with the correct form of the verb in brackets.

Winds often .... (carry) weather balloons around the earth at a height of over 24 kilometres. The instruments .... (weigh) about 40 kilos. Most weather balloons .... (measure) about 20 metres in diameter. Instruments in balloons .... (record) weather conditions. A particular one .... (measure) pollution and another radiation in the atmosphere.

Heavier-than-air machines, such as gliders and aeroplanes .... (make) a lifting force by moving through the air. This force .... (hold) them up. But balloons are lighter-than-air devices. Each one .... (move) with the air, not through it, and .... (get) its lifting force by displacement. This .... (mean) that it .... (displace) some ordinary air and .... (put) something lighter in its place, for example, hydrogen gas or hot air.

TASK FOUR

Take a sheet of paper and draw lines on it so that you have a number of boxes on the paper. Write six sentences using the present simple form and put one word in each box. Write statements, negative statements and questions. Then cut up the boxes and see how many sentences you can make with the words. If you are working with a partner, then you can exchange your words and try to make sentences with the other words.

She	goes	to	school	by	bus.
Does	John	like	football?		
Edward	doesn't	play	tennis.		

59

Winds carry weather balloons around the earth.
She still gets up at 6.30 every morning.
I think Ecuador is beautiful.

WHEN TO USE IT

We use the present simple:

(a) to state a fact or generally accepted truth:
Some vegetarians *eat* fish but they do not *eat* meat.
Winds *carry* weather balloons around the earth at a height of 24 kilometres.

(b) to talk about habits or actions that happen regularly:
Mina *plays* tennis every weekend.
She *drinks* coffee in the morning and tea in the afternoon.
The Post Office *opens* at 9.45.
Phaik Leng and Siau Jane *work* in Singapore.

(c) to express opinions:
     I think Ecuador *is* beautiful.
     He thinks engineers *are* boring.
     They *believe* everything they read.

(d) to express likes, dislikes and preferences:
     Lisette *likes* cats and dogs, but she *prefers* cats.
     Jim *prefers* coffee to tea.
     Science students *prefer* maths to languages.

COMMON EXPRESSIONS

These are informal or colloquial expressions which are usually only used in speech:

Here comes the bus/train!	This can be said when you are waiting for a train or bus and you see it approaching.
There goes my bus.	If you arrive at the bus stop as the bus is leaving and you miss it, you could say this.
That rings a bell.	I have heard that before. This is sometimes used when someone says something or says someone's name and you think you have heard it before but you can't quite remember where or when.

A. I met Jim Ball yesterday.
B. *That* name *rings a bell.* Did he live in Paris some years ago?

It's not the end of the world.   When something bad has happened you could say this to show that it isn't as bad as it seems.

A. We lost the football match.
B. Well, *it's not the end of the world*.   There's another game next week and maybe you'll win.

61

TASK ONE

Make a list of four things you like and four things you don't like. Go around the room telling people what you like and don't like and see how many people you can find who like the same things as you do and don't like the same things as you.

For example:
>   I like cats, coffee, rice and books. I don't like rats, tea, potatoes and comics.

TASK TWO

Choose three or four of the following sentences. Memorise them. Then with a partner practise saying the things and replying to what your partner says.

You:	I prefer dogs to cats.
Partner:	I prefer cats to dogs.

You:	I like tea.
Partner:	I like tea too.

You:	I think this is difficult.
Partner:	I think it's easy.

You:	I don't like snakes.
Partner:	I don't like rats.

You:	Do you think this is difficult?
Partner:	No, I don't.

You:	Does your teacher speak slowly?
Partner:	Yes, he (or she) does.
	No, she (or he) doesn't.

Now think of statements and questions of your own and work with a partner to practise them.

TASK THREE

Write what each person is saying in the following cartoons.

Unit 2.7
PRESENT CONTINUOUS
Form

Detectives are winning their fight against crime with the help of modern technology.
Nick Nolte is working hard on his movies now.
More and more people are starting to play golf in Malaysia.

HOW TO FORM IT

There are three parts to the *present continuous* form of the verb:
am, is or *are* (a form of the verb *be*)
the stem of the verb
the *-ing* ending to the stem

Be			Stem	+ *-ing* ending	Example	
I	am	[I'm]	write		I am writing.	I'm writing.
He	is	[He's]	run		He is running	He's running.
She	is	[She's]	eat		She is eating.	She's eating.
It	is	[It's]	rain	+ -ing	It is raining.	It's raining.
You	are	[You're]	study		You are studying.	You're studying.
We	are	[We're]	go		We are going.	We're going.
They	are	[They're]	play		They are playing.	They're playing.

NOTES: The present continuous form is most often used in speaking and informal writing, but it is not used very often in formal speech or writing. In speech, *am, is* and *are* are usually shortened [or contracted] to *'m, 's* or *'re*. If the verb ends in *-e*, then the *-e* is dropped before adding *-ing*:

Verb	Example
write rain run start	I am [I'm] writing a new book now. It is [It's] raining. They are [They're] running in the Marathon. More and more people are starting to play golf in Malaysia.

HOW TO FORM THE NEGATIVE

To form negative sentences, add *not* after the form of the verb *be*. You can shorten [contract] the form of the verb *be* and add it to the pronoun or noun subject and then add *not*:

It's *not* raining.

With *I* you can only use *I'm not* but with other pronouns or with nouns you can shorten [contract] *not* to *n't* and add it to the form of the verb *be*:

It *isn't* raining.
We *aren't* going.

	Be	not	Stem	+ *-ing* ending	Example	
I	am	not	write		I'm not writing.	
He	is	not	do		He's not doing the work.	He isn't doing the work.
She	is	not	eat		She's not eating.	She isn't eating
It	is	not	work	+ -ing	It's not working.	It isn't working.
You	are	not	study		You're not studying.	You aren't studying.
We	are	not	go		We're not going.	We aren't going.
They	are	not	play		They're not playing.	They aren't playing.

HOW TO FORM QUESTIONS

Put the form of the verb *be* at the beginning before the subject to make a question:
    Is it raining?

To be	Subject	Stem	+ -*ing* ending	Example
Am	I	speak		Am I speaking clearly?
	she	read		Is she reading?
Is	he	eat		Is he eating?
	it	rain	+ -*ing*	Is it raining?
	you	study		Are you studying?
Are	we	go		Are we going?
	they	play		Are they playing?

The answers can be 'Yes' or 'No' but we usually add the pronoun and a form of the verb *be*:

Am I speaking clearly?	Yes, *you are.*
Are you studying?	Yes, *I am.*
Is he eating?	No, *he isn't.*
Is she doing the work?	Yes, *she is.*
Are we going?	No, *we aren't.*
Are they playing?	Yes, *they are.*

TASK ONE

This article from a newspaper has been reproduced without the verbs that are in the present continuous form. The missing verbs are in brackets in the stem form. Fill in the blanks with the correct form of the verb.

The annual US guide to American culture was published last week and it tells us a lot about how Americans live. Nowadays, Americans .... (smoke) fewer cigarettes and .... (drink) more soft drinks. The average American .... (eat) a lot of ice-cream but .... (skip) breakfast. Perhaps because of this Americans are 30 per cent overweight. But they .... (exercise) – about 6.3 million people do exercises regularly. Nearly 11 million people jog. The statistics show that despite television Americans .... (read) more and .... (pay) more to do it.

TASK TWO

Write six sentences using a form of the present continuous. Make sure that you use

I	**we**
he, she, it	**they**
you	

at least once in your sentences.

Now rewrite your sentences but leave a blank where the verb is and put the verb in brackets in its stem form. Give your exercise to your partner and take your partner's exercise. Then see who can fill in the blanks correctly and finish first.

For example:

Your sentences
   I'm trying to improve my English.
   She's writing long sentences.

Exercise for your partner
   I .... to improve my English. (try)
   She .... long sentences. (writing)

TASK THREE

The teacher in the cartoon is trying to teach his class the rules for using the present continuous form in English. But some of the students are very bored and restless and many of them are not looking at the textbook but are doing other things.

Look at the pictures and, with your partner, ask and answer the question: 'Is she/he looking at the textbook?' Take turns asking and answering the question.

For example:
   A. Is she looking at the textbook?
   B. No, she's reading a comic.

It's raining so they have to stop the game.
More and more people are starting to play golf in Malaysia.

WHEN TO USE IT

The *present continuous* form tells us that the action is happening for a limited period of time. It can be used:

(a) to talk about something that is happening at the moment of speech:
The phone's *ringing*. I can't answer it. I'*m washing* my hair.
She's *having* lunch.
It's *raining* so they have to stop the game.

(b) to talk about something that is happening during the present period of time but may not be happening at the moment of speech or writing:
They *are writing* a new book.
She's *studying* English at the Language Centre.
He's *practising* English by listening to the radio every night.

(c) to describe a trend or something that started recently:
   More and more people *are starting* to play golf in Malaysia.
   The demand for golf course consultants *is growing*.

(d) to talk about something that is planned for the future:
   To meet the demand for English language courses, they *are planning* to expand.
   Mohan *is leaving* for London next week.
   Chin Lan *is planning* to study at Lancaster University next year.

(See Unit 2.19 for further explanations and practice.)

Verbs that can be used in the *continuous* form are called *event* verbs.

Some verbs are not usually used in the *continuous* form. These verbs are called *state* or *stative* verbs.

The verbs which do not usually have a *continuous* form are verbs of the senses which we cannot control (such as *hear, see, smell*), verbs of mental activity (such as *think, know, realise*), verbs that express feelings or emotions (such as *like, want, hate*), verbs of possession (such as *belong, own, possess*) and other verbs such as *concern, consist, contain, seem* and *matter*.

Here is a list of some common verbs that are not usually used in the *continuous* form:

be	mean
believe	need
belong	prefer
forget	realise
hate	remember
have (when the meaning is	see
'possess' or 'suffer from')	seem
hear	think (when the meaning is 'believe')
know	understand
like	want
love	

These verbs are not usually used in the *continuous* form because they do not usually mean something temporary.

If, for example, we believe or think or know something, we expect to continue to believe, think or know those things for an indefinite period. We make these statements as <u>facts</u>, not as temporary states or events.

However, when these verbs express an <u>event</u> or an <u>action</u>, or have a meaning that is connected with an action, then they can be used in the *continuous* form just as any other event verb:

   I *think* it's very difficult. (fact)
   I am *thinking* of buying a new computer. (event/action)

70

In the first example the speaker is expressing an opinion which she/he believes to be a fact which has no time limit. In the second example the speaker is using 'think' to mean 'consider' or 'plan' and knows that this planning time will end when she/he makes a decision and either does or does not buy a new computer.

WARNING BOX

Have is never used in the continuous form when it means 'suffer from':
I *have* flu.
He can't come to the meeting because he *has* a fever.

Have can be used in the continuous form when it means 'have something done':
I'*m having* my hair cut on Wednesday.
They'*re having* the house painted.

Have can be used in the continuous form when it means 'experience':
I'*m having* a lot of problems with this task.
They'*re having* trouble selling their house.

COMMON EXPRESSIONS

These expressions are used in informal spoken English.

How's it going?	This is an informal greeting which means 'How are you?', 'How are you getting on?' or 'How are you doing?'
How are you getting on?	See 'How's it going' above.
How are you doing? Also 'How is she/he getting on/doing?' 'How are they getting on/doing?'	See 'How's it going?' above.
What's going on?	This means 'What is happening?' and is usually used to ask someone for an explanation of something you do not understand. If, for example, you joined a group of people who were arguing very excitedly about something or shouting at one another, you might say 'What's going on?'
Getting over it	Recovering from something He was very unhappy about failing his exam but he's *getting over it* now.

71

Hoping for the best

Knowing that things are not good but hoping that they will get better or that the best possible thing will happen.

The news is very worrying
but we're *hoping for the best*.

Sitting on the fence

Being undecided and not taking sides in a dispute or controversy

A. How is he going to vote in the election?
B. He can't make up his mind. He's still *sitting on the fence*.

TASK ONE

Imagine that you have just met a friend you have not seen for a year. Your friend asks what you are doing these days. Make a list of the things you are doing and tell your partner.

For example:
A. What are you doing these days?
B. Well, I'm going to English classes three times a week and I'm studying very hard. I'm learning to drive; I'm building a boat...

TASK TWO

Think of the changes which have taken place in your community or your country over the past few years. Make a list of some of the changes in:

> how people spend their free time
> what people eat and drink
> what subjects are popular and unpopular in schools and universities
> any other changes in people's habits you have noticed.

Then you can either write these notes up as a report or give an oral report to a group of your colleagues in the class or to the whole class.

For example:
> More people are watching videos at home. Fewer people are going out to the cinema.

TASK THREE

Practise the common expressions explained in this Unit by answering the following questions:

(a) There's a new student in your class. You meet her outside the classroom. What could you say? What would the student say?

(b) You walk into the classroom and find three students standing by the window staring out and others gathered around the teacher's desk talking excitedly. What could you say?

(c) You have just finished doing an English test. You are not sure whether you have done well or not. What do you say to your friend when she/he asks you how you did on the test?

(d) A society you belong to has decided to donate money to the *World Wide Fund for Nature*. Four of the committee members are in favour and four are against. One member doesn't seem to be able to decide what to do. How would you describe his/ her position?

Unit 2.9
PAST SIMPLE
Form

**In 1929 the American astronomer Edwin Hubble made a surprising discovery.
John Loud invented the ballpoint pen in 1888.**

HOW TO FORM IT

Regular verbs

Most verbs are *regular*. Add *-ed* to the stem of the verb:

Subject	Stem	Ending	Example
I You She/he/it We They	play jump act finish work	+ -ed	I played football yesterday. You jumped into the water. She/he/it acted in the play. We finished our work. They worked very hard.

Examples:

Verb	Example
play jump act invent rain finish produce	I played chess with Geoff last week. You jumped over the hole in the road. Anjelica Huston acted in 'The Grifters'. John Loud invented the ballpoint pen in 1888. It rained all day yesterday. We finished our homework at 8 o'clock. In 1938 the Hungarian brothers Laszlo and Georg Biro produced a reliable ballpoint pen.

Irregular verbs

Some verbs are *irregular*. They have a different form for the past. Some common verbs with irregular past forms are:

Stem	Past form	Stem	Past form
begin	began	go	went
come	came	make	made
do	did	say	said
find	found	take	took
get	got	think	thought

Examples:

Verb	Example
go	In 1948 Auguste Piccard went over 3 kilometres down into the sea.
make	In 1929 the American astronomer Edwin Hubble made a surprising discovery.
think	In the past people thought the earth was flat.

Apart from these verbs, there are many more irregular verbs. In Appendix 1 you will find a list of the most common ones and of the past forms of these verbs.

HOW TO FORM THE NEGATIVE

To make negative sentences, add *did* and *not* before the verb stem. *Did + not* is often joined to make *didn't* in informal speech and writing:

Subject	Did not	Stem	Example	
I You She He It We They	did not [didn't]	play jump want do rain finish act	I did not play well. You did not jump. She did not want it. He did not do the work. It did not rain. We did not finish. They did not act quickly.	I didn't play well. You didn't jump. She didn't want it. He didn't do the work. It didn't rain. We didn't finish. They didn't act quickly.

HOW TO FORM QUESTIONS

Put *did* before the pronoun or subject noun and then add the stem verb to make questions:

Did	Subject	Stem	Example
Did	I you she he it we they	play jump want do rain finish act	Did I play well? Did you jump? Did she want it? Did he do the work? Did it rain there? Did we finish? Did they act quickly?

The answer to these questions can be 'Yes' or 'No' but we usually add the pronoun and *did* or *didn't* after the pronoun:

Did I play well?	Yes, *you did*.
Did you jump?	No, *I didn*'t.
Did she want it?	Yes, *she did*.
Did he do the work?	Yes, *he did*.
Did it rain here?	No, *it didn*'t.
Did we finish?	Yes, *you did*?
Did they act quickly?	No, *they didn*'t?

You can also say 'I don't know'. If you add anything after 'I don't know', then you have to use *if* + pronoun + *did*:

Did it rain there?   I don't know.
I don't know *if it did*.

TASK ONE

(a) *Fill in the correct past forms of the verb in the following chart. Some of the verbs are regular and some are irregular. Try to do it on your own first. Then look up the ones you do not know in a dictionary or in Appendix 1, or check with a partner if you are working with someone else. The first two have been done.*

Stem	Past	Stem	Past
add	*added*	leave	....
become	*became*	like	....
begin	....	live	....
break	....	love	....
bring	....	make	....
carry	....	mean	....
choose	....	need	....
come	....	play	....
decrease	....	put	....
do	....	read	....
drink	....	say	....
drive	....	see	....
eat	....	send	....
fall	....	speak	....
find	....	take	....
get	....	teach	....
go	....	think	....
hold	....	travel	....
keep	....	understand	....
know	....	want	....
laugh	....	write	....

(b) *How many regular verbs are there in the list?*

TASK TWO

Fill in the correct past form of the verb in brackets in the following passage.

In 1929 the American astronomer Edwin Hubble .... (make) a surprising discovery. He .... (find) that all the galaxies were moving away from us and from each other very fast. This .... (mean) that the whole universe was expanding like a balloon being blown up. He .... (demonstrate) this with a balloon. He .... (paint) spots on a balloon to represent the galaxies and then .... (blow) it up. The spots .... (grow) farther and farther apart.

TASK THREE

Fill in the correct form of the verb in brackets in the following passage.

A fourteen-year-old boy .... (leave) his home in Africa last month and .... (go) to Britain. He .... (leave) his family behind. His mother .... (put) him on the plane. When he .... (arrive) in London, he .... (go) to a church hall in Hackney, north London. After ten days he .... (find) a relative and he .... (move). He .... (enter) a school and .... (start) English lessons.

80

**Tom Cruise married Australian actress Nicole Kidman in January 1991.
After *Splash*, Tom Hanks made twelve comedy films.**

WHEN TO USE IT

We use the past simple:

(a) to state a fact about the past:
  In the past people *believed* that the earth was flat.
  The brazil nut *originated* in the Amazon.

(b) to talk about an event, something that happened in the past:
  John Loud *invented* the ballpoint pen in 1888.
  In 1929 the American astronomer Edwin Hubble *made* an astounding discovery.
  He *found* that all the galaxies were moving away from the earth at high speed.
  The Ming Dynasty in China *lasted* from 1368 to 1644.

(c) to talk about a state, or condition or people's habits in the past:
  When Lisette and Pete *lived* in Scotland they *had* two cats.
  I *went* to school by bus when I *was* a child.
  They *took* a lot of photographs on their holiday.

81

COMMON EXPRESSIONS

Whatever possessed you to do that?

Why did you do that? This is used only when the speaker thinks the other person has done something very stupid or strange.

A. I told my boss he was stupid.
B. *Whatever possessed you to do that?*
A. Well, he made me angry.

What did I say? or
What did I tell you?

This is said when something which the speaker predicted would happen actually happens.

A. I failed my exam.
B. *What did I tell you?*
   You didn't study hard enough!

TASK ONE

Make a list of everything you did and thought from the time you got up today until now. If you are working with a partner, ask your partner what he/she did and tell him/her what you did. Did you do the same things as your partner? If you are working in a group, report the differences.

For example:

I got up at 7.30 but .... (name of your partner) got up at 8.00. I ate toast and .... ate eggs for breakfast ....

TASK TWO

One of your friends did not come to the English class last week. Write a short note to her/him about all the things you did in class and the homework you did. You could include:

what grammar you learnt
what topics you studied
what activities you did
what homework you did, etc.

When you have written your note, work with another student and compare your two notes. Did you both include the same things?

If you are working on this book on your own, you can still do this activity and ask someone who knows English to check it for you.

TASK THREE

Practise the common expressions explained in this Unit by answering the following questions:

(a) What can you say when your friend doesn't take your advice and something bad happens?
(b) What can you say to a friend who tells you he or she has done something stupid?

Now, if you are working with another learner, make up some dialogues to practise these expressions.

Unit 2.11
PAST CONTINUOUS
Form

He was not feeling well.
She was working for British Telecom.
We were staying in a small hotel.

HOW TO FORM IT

There are three parts to the *past continuous* form of the verb:
    was or *were* (a form of the verb *be*)
    the stem of the verb
    the *-ing* ending to the stem

	Be	Stem	+ *-ing* ending	Example
I		sing		I was singing.
He		eat		He was eating.
She	was	write		She was writing.
It		rain	+ -ing	It was raining.
You		read		You were reading.
We	were	sit		We were sitting.
They		watch		They were watching.

NOTES: The past continuous form is most often used in speaking, informal writing and narrative, but it is not used very often in formal writing. If the verb ends in -e, then the -e is dropped before adding -ing:

Verb	Example
sing	I was singing in the shower.
rain	It was raining.
watch	They were watching a TV programme.
write	She was writing a poem.

HOW TO FORM THE NEGATIVE

To form negative sentences, add *not* after the form of the verb *be*:
> It *was not* raining.

You can shorten [contract] *not* to *n't* and add it to the form of the verb *be*:
> It *wasn't* raining.
> We *weren't* going.

Be	not	Stem	+ *-ing* ending	Example	
I		sing		I was not singing.	I wasn't singing.
He		eat		He was not eating.	He wasn't eating.
	was	not [wasn't]			
She		write		She was not writing.	She wasn't writing.
It		rain	+ -ing	It was not raining.	It wasn't raining.
You		read		You were not reading.	You weren't reading.
We were	not [weren't]	sit		We were not sitting.	We weren't sitting.
They		watch		They were not watching.	They weren't watching.

HOW TO FORM QUESTIONS

Put the form of the verb *be* at the beginning before the subject to form a question:
   Was it raining?

Be	Subject	Stem	+ *-ing* ending	Example
Was Were	I she he it you we they	speak listen eat run study go play	+ -ing	Was I speaking clearly? Was she listening? Was he eating? Was it running? Were you studying? Were we going? Were they playing?

The answers can be 'Yes' or 'No' but usually we add the pronoun and a form of the verb *be*:

Was I speaking clearly?	Yes, *you were.*
Were you writing a letter?	Yes, *I was.*
Was he playing?	No, *he was*n't.
Was she cooking?	Yes, *she was.*
Were we watching TV?	No, *you were*n't.
Were they playing?	Yes, *they were.*

WARNING BOX

See Units 2.7 and 2.8 for verbs that are not usually used in the *continuous* form.

86

TASK ONE

Fill in the past continuous form of the verbs in brackets in the blanks in the following passage:

When we went into the restaurant in the hotel in Sydney, there were 20 Japanese couples on their honeymoon. Most of the men .... (wear) jeans and sweatshirts. The women .... (wear) Western clothes too. They .... (order) lunch and .... (make) plans for shopping and sightseeing. All of them .... (speak) Japanese to each other but they .... (order) their lunch from the waiters in English.

I noticed one of the men .... (getting) very angry. But then his friend said something to him and everyone smiled and laughed. When we left they .... (laughing) and .... (enjoy) their lunch again.

'Why .... he .... (get) angry?' we asked the waiter. 'Because he thought his friend .... (not ordering) the right meal for him,' replied the waiter. 'But it was all right in the end.'

TASK TWO

Fill in the past continuous form of the verbs in brackets in the blanks in the following passage:

When I was 18 years old I took a trip around Europe to fill in time before university. I .... (travel) with friends and we took odd jobs to make money for our travels. In July we .... (work) in Cannes where we .... (paint) boats. I .... (spend) all my spare time drawing and one day I .... (walk) past a café when I saw Pablo Picasso. He .... (have) lunch with his wife, Jacqueline, and three other people. I was too shy to speak to him but I began to draw him. When Picasso saw what I .... (do) he began to make funny faces. He .... (stick) out his tongue .... (wave) his arms and .... (roll) his eyes. But then he stopped and sat very still so I could study him and draw his remarkable face.

PAST CONTINUOUS
Function

She was walking near her home when a dog attacked her.
I met him when he was skiing solo to the North Pole.
Once I was driving through Kenya with a friend.

WHEN TO USE IT

We use *continuous* forms of verbs in spoken, conversational English and in informal notes and letters, but we rarely use them in scientific texts or formal writing.

The *past continuous* form is used for habits and activities or events in the past just as the *present continuous* form is used for the present time. (See Units 2.7 and 2.8.) It is used especially to show that an activity was interrupted.

The *past continuous* form tells us that the action was happening for a limited period of time. It can be used:

(a) to talk about something that was happening when something else happened:
     She *was walking* near her home when a dog attacked her.
     I met him when he *was skiing* solo to the North Pole.

(b) to talk about activities in the past:
     Once I *was driving* through Kenya with a friend.

88

(c) to talk about habits in the past. When we use the *continuous* form, then we usually
     add a word like *always*:
     They *were* always *worrying* about the bills they had to pay.
     He *was* always *complaining* about something.
     When they were young they *were* always *kicking* a football around the beach.

WARNING BOX

Some verbs (see Units 2.7 and 2.8) are not usually put in the *continuous* form,
either present or past, unless they have a special meaning connected with an
event.

TASK ONE

Someone went into an office and stole a typewriter at about 4.00 in the afternoon. The next day the police are questioning the four people who work in this office. They want to know what everyone was doing when the crime took place. Fill in the blanks in the following conversation with the correct form of the verb in brackets.

Police:	What .... (you do) at 4 o'clock yesterday afternoon?
Secretary:	I .... (photocopying) this report.
Police:	How long .... (you work) in the photocopy room?
Secretary:	For about an hour.
Police:	What .... (you do) at 4 o'clock yesterday afternoon?
Assistant:	I .... (stamp) the letters for the afternoon post.
Police:	Where .... (you do) this?
Assistant:	I .... (use) the franking machine in my room.
Police:	What .... (you do) at 4 o'clock yesterday afternoon?
Manager:	I .... (get) a cup of coffee.
Police:	Why didn't your secretary get the coffee?
Manager:	She .... (copy) the report so she was too busy.
Police:	What .... (you do) at 4 o'clock yesterday afternoon?
Salesperson:	I .... (write) a report and .... (telephone) some customers.
Police:	Where .... (you work)?
Salesperson:	In my office.
Police:	Did you see anyone come into the office?
Secretary:	No, I .... (look) out of the window.
Manager:	I .... (kick) the coffee machine because it .... (not work) properly.
Assistant:	No, I .... (adjust) the franking machine.
Salesperson:	No, I .... (not look) at the door. I .... (type) my report and I .... (look up) numbers in the telephone directory.
Police:	Did anyone hear anything?
All:	No, the photocopier .... (make) too much noise.

90

TASK TWO

Make notes of the things you did at different times in the past three days. Put something down for
8.00, 10.00, 12.00, 2.00, 4.00, 6.00, 8.00.

Work with a partner if you can and ask him or her what she/he was doing at each of those times on
each of the past three days. (If you are working on your own, write the questions and answers and
ask someone to check them for you.)

For example:

Friday	Saturday	Sunday
8.00: having a shower	reading the paper	having coffee in bed
10.00: meeting my boss	washing the dog	making breakfast

Ask your partner:

What were you doing at 10.00 on Sunday morning?
Your partner will answer and ask you what you were doing at another or the same time.

How many times were you and your partner doing the same thing?

Unit 2.13
TALKING ABOUT THE FUTURE

There is no future tense as such in English but there are many ways of talking about the future. In this book we will deal with only four of these ways:

Will/shall + stem [infinitive]:
He'll *be* here at 5 o'clock.

Be going to + stem [infinitive]:
She'*s going to buy* a new computer.

Present continuous form:
The British Council *is moving* to a new building next year.

Present simple form:
The train *leaves* at 7.15.

In Units 2.14 to 2.19 we will look at each of these ways of talking about the future.

Unit 2.14
FUTURE:
WILL/SHALL + STEM
Form

They'll be here soon.
We'll be back in a few minutes.
She'll finish her exams on Friday.

HOW TO FORM IT

The most common way to talk about the future is to use *will* or *shall* or the short form [contraction] *'ll*.

The use of *shall* is no longer very common in English. Learners used to be taught that *shall* was used for the pronouns *I* and *we* and *will* was used for the other pronouns or subjects, *he, she, it, you, they*. In modern English, however, *shall* is not used very often. In usual speech and informal writing, the most common form is the short form *'ll* after the subject:
   I'*ll*, you'*ll*, she'*ll*, we'*ll*, they'*ll*.

Subject	Will		Stem	Example
I	will	[I'll]	see	I'll see you tomorrow.
You	will	[You'll]	find	You'll find it on page 71.
She	will	[She'll]	finish	She'll finish it later.
He	will	[He'll]	do	He'll do it next week.
It	will	[It'll]	be	It'll be ready at 5.30.
We	will	[We'll]	have	We'll have dinner at 7.30.
They	will	[They'll]	work	They'll work on the report next week.

HOW TO FORM THE NEGATIVE

When we join *will* + *not* it usually becomes *won't*:

    I *will not* do it. I *won't* do it.

Subject	Will not	Stem	Example
I You . She He It We They	will not [won't]	finish fail lose go start be come	I won't finish this today. You won't fail the exam. She won't lose her job. He won't go to the party. The engine won't start. We won't be there tomorrow. They won't come on time.

HOW TO FORM QUESTIONS

Will	Subject	Stem	Example
Will	I you she he it we they	get be catch be break finish come	Will I get an A in the exam? Will you be here for the meeting? Will she catch the early train? Will he be angry? Will it break? Will we finish today? Will they come to the party?

The answers can be 'Yes' or 'No' but we usually add the pronoun + *will* to yes answers, and the pronoun + *won't* to 'No' answers:

    Will I get an A in the exam?   Yes, *you will.*

    Will you be here for the meeting?   No, *I won't.*

You can also say 'I don't know'. If you add anything after 'I don't know', then you have to use 'if + pronoun + *will*':

    Will they come to the party?   I don't know.

    Will she finish in time?   I don't know *if she will.*

You can also say 'I don't think so or 'I don't think + pronoun + *will*':

    Will it break?   I don't think so.

        I don't think it *will.*

Or, you can use a word like 'probably' or 'possibly':

    Will we finish today?   Yes, probably.

        Yes, we probably *will* (finish).

    Will he be angry?   Yes, possibly.

TASK ONE

*Answer the following questions. Use **Yes** or **No** + pronoun + **will/won't**.*

For example:
Will the train be on time? Yes it will.
Will John be at the meeting? No, he won't.

(a) Will you be here tomorrow?
(b) Will the weather be fine on Sunday?
(c) Will they give a party for the class?
(d) Will there be time to finish the project?
(e) Will we be able to see him?
(f) Will the children be on holiday next week?
(g) Will the staff get a holiday on Monday?
(h) Will Sandra change her mind about the party?
(i) Will Simon go to the Lake District with us?
(j) Will I be successful?

TASK TWO

Ask questions about the following topics.

For example:
go to the theatre.
You: Will she go to the theatre with us?
come to a party.
You: Will you come to a party on Saturday?

(a) finish before 6 o'clock
(b) see Margaret and Carole
(c) catch the early train
(d) sit at the front of the bus
(e) find a cure for cancer
(f) finish the experiment
(g) use more than two tins of paint
(h) Real Madrid win the match
(i) air travel be cheaper in the future
(j) the government increase taxes

TASK THREE

*Answer the questions you asked in TASK TWO. Use **Yes** or **No** + pronoun + **will/won't**. You can do this orally with a partner or write down the answers.*

95

Computer technology will influence our future.

In less than 10 years we will be writing the date 1.1.2000.

The winner of this match will play in the finals on Wednesday.

WHEN TO USE IT

We use this form for the future:

(a) to make predictions about the future or ask questions about the future:
Computer technology *will influence* our future.
In less than ten years we *will be writing* the date 1.1.2000.
The winner of this match *will play* in the finals on Wednesday.
Will the government *call* an election this year?

(b) to state decisions that you have just made and that haven't been planned:
I'll finish this report tomorrow.
I think *I'll have* a sandwich for lunch.

(c) to make a promise:
I'll phone you next week.
I'll be here at 9.00 tomorrow.

(d) to invite someone to do something:
Will you *come* to my house on Sunday?
Will you *come* to the cinema with us?

(e) to offer to do something for someone:
I'll cook the dinner tonight.
I'll help you with your essay.
I'll wash the dishes and you can dry them.

NOTE: Another way to offer to do something is to ask a question with *shall*. This is one time when *shall* is always used with *I* and *We*:
Shall I *carry* those books for you?
Shall we *come* early and help you get ready for the party?

COMMON EXPRESSIONS

Will you stop doing that! Will you shut up!	This is used to tell someone to do something. It is not very polite and can only be used in informal situations. It is often used when speaking to children. In this expression *will* is always stressed (or emphasised).
He *will* play his music too loud!	Here *will* is also stressed. It means that someone always behaves in a particular way and won't change his ways.

TASK ONE

*Make a list of ten changes that you think will take place in your country in the next ten years. Then tell your partner or write these down using the **will/shall + stem (infinitive)** form.*

For example:

> In 2002 there will be fewer private cars in Britain.
> In 2004 everyone will work 30 hours a week.

TASK TWO

*Using either **I'll + stem (infinitive)** or **Shall I + stem**, offer to help the people described below.*

For example:

> A shopper is trying to reach a loaf of bread on a high shelf.
> *You:* 'Shall I get it for you?'
> You are at a friend's house. The friend is busy cooking when the phone rings.
> *You:* 'I'll answer it.'

(a) An old man is carrying a heavy shopping bag.
(b) A young child is trying to reach a book on a high shelf in the library.
(c) Some friends tell you that they are painting their flat.
(d) Your teacher is cleaning the board.
(e) A motorist is trying to get the car to start.
(f) Your friend says she has left her money at home and can't buy a cup of coffee.
(g) Your neighbour's cat is stuck in a tree.
(h) Your friends plan to go to a party but they can't get anyone to look after their children.
(i) Your teacher has a lot of books and papers to hand out to the class.
(j) You see a small child crying in a crowded supermarket.

TASK THREE

Fill in the missing parts in the following dialogues using **will/shall + stem (infinitive)**.

(a) *Jane:* You've been working all morning. When are you going to have lunch?
     Patricia: Okay. ....

(b) *George:* I've got an exam on Monday but I haven't finished typing my report.
     Paul: ....

(c) *Chris:* The neighbours are making a lot of noise.
     Jim: ....

(d) *Pete:* Look, I know you are trying to work but I really want to tell you about what
     happened to me.
     Edward: ....

(e) *Carol:* I really need some help with this.
     Paula: Don't worry. ....

Unit 2.16
FUTURE:
BE + GOING TO + STEM
Form

They're going to make the film in Bangkok.
She's going to retire from politics.
He's going to play in the chess tournament.

HOW TO FORM IT

A common way of expressing the future is *be* + ***going to*** + ***stem***:

Subject	Be Not		Going to	Stem	Example
I	am	[I'm]		watch	I'm going to watch a film.
You	are	[You're]		pass	You're going to pass the exam.
She	is	[She's]		retire	She's going to retire from politics.
He	is	[He's]	going to	play	He's going to play chess.
It	is	[It's]		come	It's going to come on time.
We	are	[We're]		fly	We're going to fly to Oporto.
They	are	[They're]		make	They're going to make the film in Bangkok.

HOW TO FORM THE NEGATIVE

To form a negative sentence, put *not* before *going to*. There are two ways of shortening [contracting] the forms. You can either shorten the form of the verb *be* and add it to the pronoun or noun subject:

You*'re not going to* win.

Or shorten *not* to *n't* and add it to the form of the verb *be*:

You *aren't going to* win.

100

With *I*, you can only shorten *am* to *'m* and add it to I:
   I'm not going to win.

Subject	Be	Not	Going to	Stem	Example
I	am			play	I'm not going to play.
You	are			fall	You're not going to fall.
					You aren't going to fall.
She	is			come	She's not going to come.
		not	going to		She isn't going to come.
He	is			move	He's not going to move.
					He isn't going to move.
We	are			try	We're not going to try.
					We aren't going to try.
They	are			win	They're not going win.
					They aren't going win.

HOW TO FORM QUESTIONS

Put the form of the verb *be* before the subject to form a question. This is similar to the way as we make questions with the present continuous form of the verb:

Be	Subject	Going to	Stem	Example
Am	I		be	Am I going to be late?
Are	you		watch	Are you going to watch the film?
Is	she		come	Is she going to come to the party?
Is	he	going to	buy	Is he going to buy a new car?
Is	it		be	Is it going to be ready today?
Are	we		meet	Are we going to meet the President?
Are	they		play	Are they going to play tennis?

The answer to the question can be 'Yes', 'No' but we usually add the pronoun and the form of the verb *be*:
   Is she going to the party?   Yes, she *is*.
   Are they going to play tennis?   No, they*'re* not. No, they *aren't*.

If you say 'I don't know' you do not need to add the pronoun and the form of the verb *be* unless you also add *if*:
   Are you going to watch the film?   I don't know.
                                       I don't know *if we are*.

TASK ONE

*Answer the following questions with **Yes, No** or **I don't know.***

For example:

Are they going to buy that house?   Yes, they are.
Is she going to join the society?   No, she's not./No, she isn't.
Are you going to go on holiday?   I don't know.
                                     I don't know if we are.

(a) Are you going to do your homework?
(b) Is she going to buy a computer?
(c) Are they going to play football on Saturday?
(d) Is Brazil going to win the World Cup?
(e) Are we going to finish this book?
(f) Are you going to buy a car this year?
(g) Is it going to rain?
(h) Are they going to have a party?
(i) Is the cat going to have kittens?
(j) Is she going to stop smoking?

TASK TWO

In the following task, the answers to the questions are given. Write the questions in the blanks.

For example:

Q. **Are you going to finish the report today?**

A. Yes, I am. I'm on the last page.

Q. **Are they going to get a cat?**

A. No, they aren't. He doesn't like cats.

(a) Q. ....?
     A. Yes, I'm on page 375.

(b) Q. ....?
     A. It probably is. The sky is very dark.

(c) Q. ....?
     A. Yes, he has £600.

102

(d) *Q.* .... ?

     A. No, she isn't. She doesn't like concerts.

(e) *Q.* .... ?

     A. No, they aren't. They're too busy.

(f) *Q.* .... ?

     A. Yes, probably. She needs a new one.

(g) *Q.* .... ?

     A. No, they aren't. They're going to watch a video.

(h) *Q.* .... ?

     A. Probably. It's a nice day.

(i) *Q.* .... ?

     A. I don't know. It's very expensive.

(j) *Q.* .... ?

     A. Yes, I am. I like baking bread.

Unit 2.17
FUTURE:
BE + GOING TO + STEM
Function

There isn't going to be an election this year in Britain.
We're going to live in Madeira when we retire.

WHEN TO USE IT

We use form *be + going to + stem (infinitive)*:

(a) to make predictions about the future. When we make predictions we can use either *be + going to + stem (infinitive)* or *will + stem (infinitive)*. The form *be + going to + stem (infinitive)* is less formal than the *will + stem (infinitive)* form and is more common in speech than in writing:

> There *isn't going to be* an election this year.
> The economic situation *is going to get* worse.

WARNING BOX

Although we often start with *be + going to + stem (infinitive)* at the beginning of a passage, we continue with *will + stem (infinitive)*:

> A. What *are* you *going to do* about the problem?
> B. Well, I'm *going to study* the whole problem very carefully. And then I'*ll spend* some time consulting other people and finally I'*ll make* a decision.

(See Units 2.14 and 2.15 for *will/shall + stem*.)

(b) to talk about a plan that has already been made. This is different from a prediction because the speaker or writer is not guessing but stating what has already been decided:

> We'*re going to live* in Madeira when we retire.
> Imperial College, London, *is going to recruit* twelve new academics to build up its research on environmental science.
> He *is going to learn* Spanish before he moves to Spain.

104

(c) to say that something is going to happen in the future because of or as a result of something that is true in the present time:

It's *going to rain*. (because the sky is very dark and there is thunder)

She's *going to be* very happy. (because she's going to hear some good news)

WARNING BOX

We cannot use *be + going to + stem (infinitive)* to make an offer or to say that someone is willing to do something. For these we have to use *will/shall + stem (infinitive)*:

This is very heavy. *Shall* I *help* you move it?

A. I don't know how to do this.

B. Ask Joan. She'*ll show* you how to do it.

In the first example someone is making an offer to help. In the second example, someone is saying that Joan is willing to help.

TASK ONE

Fill in the correct form of the verb in the blanks in the passages below.

(a) *Interviewer:* What are your plans for the future?

    Oliver Stone: I .... (not continue) with the film *Evita*. Instead, I ....
    (start) on a film about the killing of John F. Kennedy.

(b) *Interviewer:* What .... you .... (do) in the future?

    Tom Hanks: The future? I .... (learn to speak) French, ... (learn to
    play) the piano, ... (move) to California, ... (ride) a raft
    down a long river and .... (play) Iago in Shakespeare's
    'Othello'.

TASK TWO

Before you do this task you should look at Units 1.5 and 1.6 on Questions.

People's plans for the future

If you have a partner then work with him or her. One of you should look at the picture so you can answer the questions. The other should only ask questions about the people listed below. After one of you has asked a number of questions, change places with your partner and answer the questions. If you are working on your own, then you can write the questions and answers and check with the suggested answers at the back of the book.

For example:

    Q: What is Paul going to do next year?

    A: He's going to buy a Rolls Royce.

TASK THREE

Write down some of the things you plan to do in the next week
month
year
five years.

Then tell your partner about your plans and ask about his or her plans.

For example:

I'm going to paint the house this summer. Are you going to do anything with your house?

107

The plane leaves at 6.00.
The film starts at 9.30.
The party is on Friday.

HOW TO FORM IT

For *I, you, we, they* use the simple stem of the verb:
   I *play*
   you *play*
   we *play*
   they *play*

For he, she and *it* add -*s* to the stem:
   he *plays*
   she *plays*
   it *plays*

See Unit 2.5 (Present simple) for a complete summary of how to form it.

WHEN TO USE IT

We use the *present simple* form to talk about the future when the event is a definite fact. This is because the *present simple* form is used to express facts either in the present time or for the future:

   Tomorrow *is* Wednesday.
The calendar is fixed and we know what order the days come in.

   The plane *leaves* at 6.00.
Airline schedules are set many months ahead so times of planes (and buses and trains) are fixed.

   The film *starts* at 9.30.
Again, film schedules are always fixed ahead of time.

108

The party *is* on Friday.
This is seen as a fact because it was planned some time ago.

These are all identified as facts and not as possible events.

WARNING BOX

We very often use the *present simple* form to talk about the future but this is usually in dependent clauses after conditionals such as *if* or *unless* (see Units 2.34, 2.35 and 2.36) or after time conjunctions such as *when, as soon as, until,* etc. The verb in the main clause is usually in the *will/shall* or *'ll* form or the *be going to +
stem (infinitive)* form, but the verb in the dependent clause introduced by *if, unless, when,* etc. is in the *present simple* or *present continuous* form:

What will we do about the picnic if it *rains*?
I'll call you as soon as I *have* time.
I'm going to finish this when I*'m* on holiday.

109

TASK ONE

Fill in the blanks with the correct form of the verb in brackets in the following sentences.

(a) I'm going to buy a video as soon as I .... (have) enough money.
(b) The plane .... (arrive) at 5.00 in the morning.
(c) I'm going to take a tape recorder to use when I .... (be) in the Far East.
(d) The film .... (start) at 7.30 so we have to leave here at 7.00.
(e) What time does the train for London .... (leave)?
(f) What .... (be) on TV tonight?
(g) What day of the week .... (be) your birthday this year?
(h) The play .... (start) at 7.30. What time does it .... (end)?
(i) My exams .... (finish) on Tuesday.
(j) The wedding .... (be) on Saturday.

TASK TWO

Try to make as many correct and interesting sentences with the following words. Use one word from each column. You can make statements, questions or negative sentences. You can add any words you like but you must use one word from each column in each sentence.

I	do	me	if	speak
you	come	you	when	tell
she	ask	her	as soon as	go
he	play	him	after	see
it	have	it	before	rain
we	arrive	us	until	leave
they	stay	them	unless	telephone
your name	get	Partner's name	till	finish

For example:

> I'll see her when I arrive.
> I'll play with my daughter when I finish this.
> We'll stay with you when we go to Corfu.
> Will you ask him when you telephone him?
> They won't come if it rains.

110

He's leaving next week.
They're moving into a new office next month.
They're going to Yugoslavia for their honeymoon.

HOW TO FORM IT

There are three parts to this form of the verb:
  am, is or *are* (a form of the verb *be*)
  the stem of the verb
  the *-ing* ending the stem.

See Unit 2.7 (Present continuous) for a complete summary of how to form it.

WHEN TO USE IT

We can talk about the future by using the *present continuous* form. This is considered to be an informal spoken form and it is not often used in formal writing.

The meaning is almost the same as the meaning of *be going to + stem (infinitive)*. It means that something is going to happen quite soon. We usually add a word or phrase that says when it is going to happen. If you do not add a time phrase or something that shows that it is in the future, then people might think you were talking about the present time:

He's *leaving* next week.
They're *getting* married in May.
They're *visiting* Venice during their honeymoon.
They're *moving* into a new office next month.
We're *meeting* after work.
She's *eating* sandwiches for lunch.

111

The important thing to remember about the *present continuous* form when it is used to talk about the future is that it has one basic meaning. It always refers to a future event that will happen because of a present or agreed plan or decision.

Another important point to remember is that the future event must be planned by human beings.
You cannot say:

* It *is raining* tomorrow.
   or
* The flowers *are blooming* next month.

Many people think that their pets are like people and use the *present continuous* form to talk about their future actions:

Her cat *is having* kittens next week.

WARNING BOX

The *present continuous* form to indicate the future can only be used for events, not with state verbs (see Unit 2.8) which cannot take the *-ing* form. With state verbs, we have to use the *will/shall* or *'ll + stem (infinitive)* form or the *be going to + stem (infinitive)* form:

There *will be* no class tomorrow.
It's *going to be* very difficult to get there on time.

COMMON EXPRESSIONS

There are many combinations of *go + noun* or *noun phrase* or *preposition/adverb*.
With these expressions we often put *go* in the *present continuous* form to talk about future plans:

go shopping
go out
go to bed
go away
go on holiday

You could use the *going to* form for the future (*I'm going to go shopping*, *He's going to go out*) but we usually say:

I'm *going shopping*.
He's *going out*.
The child *is going* to bed.
They're *going away*.
She's *going on holiday*.
We're *going swimming/skiiing/hiking/walking*.

TASK ONE

*Put the correct form of the verbs (form of **be** + ... **-ing**) in brackets in the following passages. All of the events are in the future.*

(a) Everyone who .... (buy) a present for a child this Christmas should check very carefully that it is safe.

(b) Gary Lineker .... (fly) to Japan to raise money for his club.

(c) What .... (you, do) next week? I .... (play) in a chess competition.

(d) Who .... (meet) us at the airport tomorrow?

(e) We .... (move) house next week.

(f) He .... (go) to Crete on holiday next month.

(g) Who .... (play) in the finals next week?

(h) They .... (get) married in November.

(i) The judges .... (announce) the winners at the dinner tonight.

(j) We .... (have) a bring-a-dish supper tonight. Everyone .... (bring) a different dish. The guests .... (arrive) at 7.30 and we .... (eat) at 8.00.

TASK TWO

Write down one thing you are planning to do this evening. Then ask your colleagues what they plan to do and answer their questions about your plans.

For example:

  What are you doing this evening? I'm staying home and watching TV.

Unit 2.20
PRESENT PERFECT
Form

She has lived in Seville since she was eleven.
Bob Dylan has made three films.
The monsoon has started in Malaysia.

HOW TO FORM IT

The *present perfect* form of the verb is made up of *has/have 's/'ve* + past participle:
  He *has changed*.
  They *have gone*.

The past participle form of regular verbs is stem + *-ed*. In Appendix 1 you will find a list of the past participle forms of irregular verbs.

In spoken English we often shorten [contract] *has* or *have* and join it to the subject noun or pronoun:
  I *have seen* the film. I*'ve seen* it.
  She *has finished* it. She*'s finished* her book.

In written English we usually use the full form unless we are writing informal notes or letters.

114

Subject	Has/Have	Past Participle	Example
I	have [I've]	been	I have been to Cuenca. I've been to Cuenca.
You	have [You've]	worked	You have worked hard. You've worked hard.
We	have [We've]	lived	We have lived here for three years. We've lived here for three years.
They	have [They've]	made	They have made a film. They've made a film.
She	has [She's]	taken	She has taken her medicine. She's taken her medicine.
He	has [He's]	written	He has written a book. He's written a book.
It	has [It's]	changed	It has changed my life. It's changed my life.

HOW TO FORM THE NEGATIVE

To form negative sentences, add *not* after *have* or *has*. There are two ways of shortening [contracting] the negative. You can either shorten *not* to *n't* and join it to *have* or *has*:

I *haven't been* to Brasilia.
She *hasn't seen* the film.

Or, shorten the form of the verb *have* and add it to the noun or pronoun subject:

I*'ve not been* to Brasilia.
She*'s not seen* the film.

If you do this, the *not* stands out and the sentence can sound more emphatic. It is not a very common form.

Subject	Has/Have	not	Past participle	Example
I			been	I haven't been to Cascaes.
You	have	not [haven't]	finished	You haven't finished yet.
We			seen	We haven't seen the film.
They			written	They haven't written the report.
She			left	She hasn't left yet.
He	has	not [hasn't]	fed	He hasn't fed the cats.
It			made	It hasn't made any difference.

HOW TO FORM QUESTIONS

Put *have* or *has* in front of the subject to make a question:

Has/Have	Subject	Past participle	Example
Have	I	met	Have I met you before?
	you	finished	Have you finished your dinner?
	we	agreed	Have we agreed on a plan?
	they	built	Have they built the house?
Has	she	been	Has she been to Bangalore?
	he	seen	Has he seen the President?
	it	left	Has the train left?

The answer to these questions can be 'Yes' or 'No' but we usually add the pronoun and *have* or *has* to the answer. You cannot shorten [contract] *has/have* in the answer:

Have you finished your dinner?   Yes, I *have*.
                                 No, I *haven't*.
Have we agreed on a plan?   Yes, we *have*.
                                 No, *we haven't* yet.
Has the train left?   Yes, *it has*.
                                 No, *it hasn't*.

You can also say 'I don't know'. If you add anything after 'I don't know', then you have to use 'if + pronoun + *have/has*':

> Have they built the house?   I don't know.
>   I don't know *if they have.*

You can also say 'I think so' or 'I think + pronoun + *have/has* (or 'I don't think . . .'):

> Has he seen the President?   I think so.
>   I think *he has.*
> Have we met before?   I don't think so.
>   I don't think *we have.*

PRESENT PERFECT CONTINUOUS

HOW TO FORM IT

There are three parts to the *present perfect continuous* form:

> *has/have* ['s/'ve] + *been* + present participle (the *-ing* form):

Subject	Has/Have	Been	Present participle	Example
I		been [I've been]	working	I've been working here for two years.
You	have	been [You've been]	waiting	You've been waiting for an hour.
We		been [We've been]	studying	We've been studying for three hours.
They		been [They've been]	playing	They've been playing since 3 o'clock.
She		been [She's been]	learning	She's been learning English for six years.
He	has	been [He's been]	running	He's been running for two hours.
It		been [It's been]	raining	It's been raining for a week.

117

HOW TO FORM THE NEGATIVE

To form negative sentences, add *not* after *have* or *has*. There are two ways of shortening [contracting] the negative. We usually shorten *not* to *n't* and join it to *have* or *has*. This is common in spoken English but we don't use it for writing unless it is very informal notes or letters to friends:

Subject	Has/Have	not	Been	Present participle	Example
I You We They	have	not [haven't]	been	feeling studying going working	I haven't been feeling well. You haven't been studying. We haven't been going out much. They haven't been working.
She He It	has	not [hasn't]		sleeping coming raining	She hasn't been sleeping well. He hasn't been coming lately. It hasn't been raining much.

Or, you can shorten the form of the verb *have* and add it to the noun or pronoun subject:

You*'ve not been studying* very hard.

She*'s not been sleeping* well recently.

But this form is considered to be formal and is not very common. It is better to use the first form.

HOW TO FORM QUESTIONS

Put *have* or *has* before the subject to make a question:

Has/Have	Subject	Been	Present participle	Example
Have	I		doing	Have I been doing well in my work?
	you		waiting	Have you been waiting here long?
	we		working	Have we been working too late this week?
	they	been	eating	Have they been eating out a lot lately?
Has	she		travelling	Has she been travelling a lot this year?
	he		feeling	Has he been feeling unwell?
	it		snowing	Has it been snowing in Moscow?

The answers to these questions can be either 'Yes' or 'No' but we usually add the pronoun and *have* or *has (been)* to the answer.

You cannot shorten [contract] *has/have* in the answer:

Have I been doing well in my work?	Yes, you *have (been)*.
Have you been waiting long?	No, I *haven't (been)*.
Has she been travelling a lot this year?	Yes, she *has (been)*.
Has he been feeling unwell?	No, he *hasn't (been)*.

You can also say 'I don't know'. If you add anything after 'I don't know', then you have to use 'if + pronoun + *have/has (been)*':

Have they been eating out a lot lately?	I don't know.
	I don't know *if they have (been)*.

You can also say 'I think so' or 'I think + pronoun + *have/has (been)*' (or, I don't think . . .'):

Has it been snowing in Moscow?	I think so.
	I think *it has (been)*.
Have we been working too hard this week?	I don't think so.
	I don't think *you have (been)*.

119

TASK ONE

Write the correct forms of the present perfect for the following verbs. Use the pronoun subjects given.

For example:	**Positive**	**Negative**	**Questions**
I ....(have)	I have had	I haven't had	Have I had .... ?
(a) You ....(see)	....	....	....
(b) They ....(be)	....	....	....
(c) She ....(go)	....	....	....
(d) It ....(rain)	....	....	....
(e) You ....(run)	....	....	....
(f) We ....(wait)	....	....	....
(g) He ....(play)	....	....	....
(h) I ....(want)	....	....	....
(i) They ....(walk)	....	....	....
(j) She ....(have)	....	....	....
(k) You ....(stay)	....	....	....
(l) I ....(think)	....	....	....
(m) We ....(sell)	....	....	....
(n) He ....(sing)	....	....	....
(o) She ....(win)			

120

TASK TWO

Complete these sentences with the correct form of the present perfect:

(a) I .... (not be) to Australia or New Zealand but my sister .... (go) to live in Sydney so I may go there next year.

(b) She .... (live) in Madras for 10 years but now she .... (decide) to move to Singapore.

(c) Mordecai Richler .... (write) more than ten novels and .... (win) the Commonwealth Writers Prize.

(d) Life .... (become) much easier in the past year.

(e) I had my nose reshaped and this .... (change) my life. I have more self-confidence than I .... (have) since I was a child.

(f) Paul Simon's album 'Rhythm of the Saints' .... (sell) more than 2 million copies in America.

(g) He .... (live) on Madeira since he was three years old. A number of British .... (settle) there.

(h) Scientists .... (study) many pairs of identical twins, especially twins who .... (live) separate lives because of adoption.

(i) Pop stars and other famous people .... (help) to raise millions of pounds for charity.

(j) The Europa Centre in Essex, England, is helping English students to use the French and German they .... (learn) at school in a new and interesting way.

```
┌─────────────────────────────────┐
│  ┌───────────────────────────┐  │
│  │        Unit 2.21          │  │
│  │   PRESENT PERFECT         │  │
│  │       Function            │  │
│  └───────────────────────────┘  │
└─────────────────────────────────┘
```

I have lived in Madeira since I was three years old.
I've met a lot of people and have done things I only dreamed about before.
They've been in London for two years.

WHEN TO USE IT

Many students of English find it difficult to know when to use the *present perfect* form of the verb in English. This is because there is no similar form in their languages or because in their languages the present simple or past simple is used to express the meaning the present perfect form has in English:

> I've *been* here for a week.
> They've *lived* in Penang since 1985.

In these two examples, there are many languages which would use the present simple to express the idea. But this is not possible in English.

If I say:

> I am here for a week. (present simple)

then I am saying that I will be here for a week from now. In other words, I have just arrived and I will be staying for a week.

But, if I say:

> I've *been* here for a week. (present perfect)

then I am saying that I came one week ago and I have been here for the past week.

> They live in Penang. (present simple)

means that they live in Penang now. But it does not tell us how long they have lived there.

> They've *lived* in Penang since 1985.

means that they have lived there for all the years from 1985 to the present.

The important thing to remember about the *present perfect* form is that it is a *present* tense. It is a bridge that joins the past to the present. But the focus is on *now*, the moment of speaking or writing.

122

There are three main uses or meanings of the verb form:

(a) a state from the past up to the present time:
   It *has been* very hot all week (and it is still very hot).
   He *has been* ill for a week (and he is still ill).

(b) events in a period leading up to the present time:
   He *has bought* a new car (so now he has a new car).
   They *have been* to Mexico but they *haven't been* to South America (so they know something about Mexico but they don't have any firsthand experience of South America.

This use of the *present perfect* form shows that it is the result of the event or action in the present which is important. When the event happened is not important.

WARNING BOX

The *present perfect* form is used when we are interested in the present time. The event we are talking about happened at some time in the past but the exact time is not important and is not mentioned. If we give the time in the past, then we are talking about when the event happened and we have to use the *past simple* form:
   They went to Mexico in 1989.
   He bought a car last week.

In these sentences we cannot use the *present perfect* form.

(c) habits or recurrent events in a period leading up to the present time:
   She *has studied* English for four years (and is still studying English now).
   Brazil *has won* the World Cup three times.

PRESENT PERFECT CONTINUOUS

WHEN TO USE IT

This form is also a present time form. It is focused on *now*, the time of speaking or writing.

We use the *present perfect continuous* form to talk about events or states that started in the past and have continued for some time and are still present at the moment of speaking or writing.

> It *has been raining* for two days (and it's still raining).
> They*'ve been waiting* for three hours (and they're still waiting now).
> He*'s been feeling* depressed for two months.

The difference between using the *continuous* form and the *non-continuous* form is that the *continuous* form stresses or emphasises the duration of the event or habit.

Some verbs, like *live, sleep, rain, sit, wait, learn* and *work* refer to actions that continue for some time. These verbs can be used in either the *continuous* or *non-continuous* form without much change in meaning:

> She *has been studying* for three years.   She has studied for three years.
> He *has been living* here for six months.   He has lived here for six months.

There is very little difference in meaning between these pairs.

USING ADVERBIALS WITH THE PRESENT PERFECT

There are some adverbials which we often use with the *present perfect* forms. These include **since, so far, ever**:

> Mordecai Richler *hasn't won* the Booker Prize *so far* but he has won the Commonwealth Writers Prize.
> There *have been* 92 road accidents *since* the beginning of the year.
> *Have* you *ever been* to Czechoslovakia?

Never can be used with either the *present*, the *past simple* or the *present perfect* forms:

> He never eats meat. (present)
> She never listened to pop music when she was young. (past simple)
> I*'ve* never *seen* a purple cow. (present perfect)

For can be used with either the *present perfect* forms or the *past simple* forms:

> John *has been* Director of the Institute for two years. (present perfect)
> Jane *has been working* on her thesis for two years. (present perfect continuous)
> Jane worked on her thesis for three years. (past simple)

124

Since (when it is a time adverbial) can only be used with the *present perfect* forms:
> They've *been working* on the building since May. (present perfect continuous)
> They *haven't seen* him since 1989. (present perfect)

NOTE: *Since* can also mean *because*. When it means *because*, it can be used with any verb form.

FOR OR SINCE?

The adverbials *for* and *since* sometimes cause problems for learners. *For* can be used with either the *past simple* form or one of the *perfect* forms, but *since* can only be used with one of the *perfect* forms.

For means during or for a *period* of time:
> He studied at Lancaster University for a year. (past simple)
> They *have been* in Portugal for three months. (present perfect)
> The cost of computers *has been dropping* for the past twelve months. (present perfect continuous)

Since means from or since a *point* in time in the past:
> He hasn't ridden a bicycle since he was 25.
> Ever since she was a teenager, Angela has been worried about it.
> They have travelled everywhere in Europe since they bought a caravan.
> He hasn't had an accident since he started racing.

The verb that comes after *since* must be in the *past simple* if it refers to a *point time in the past*. However, you could say:
> He hasn't been ill since he *has been taking* the pills. (present perfect continuous)

WARNING BOX

Remember, you cannot use the adverbial *ago* with the *present perfect* forms. *Ago* can only be used with the *past simple* form.

Remember, you can ask 'Have you ever been to Malacca?' but you cannot say
* 'I have *ever* been to Jamaica.'

NOTE: In American English, the *past simple* is often used instead of the *present perfect*, especially with such adverbials as *just, yet, already* and *recently*:

American: We just phoned him.
She just finished her work.
British: We've just spoken to him.
She hasn't done it yet.

TASK ONE

Put the correct form of the present perfect of the verbs in brackets in the blanks in the following passages.

(a) Spain and its people .... (make) a lasting impression on me. I went there as a young journalist 70 years ago and stayed for two years. Since then I .... (return) often. I .... (never forget) my first sight of the plateau of Castille and the mountains that cross it. I .... (be) to every part of the country and .... (visit) every large city in the country. Since I first fell in love with the country in 1920 I .... (be) a regular visitor and I .... (never be) disappointed.

(b) Robert Zimmerman changed his name to Bob Dylan but he .... (also call) himself Tedham Porterhouse, Elmer Johnson, Robert Milkwood and Blind Boy Grunt. He .... (receive) a doctorate from Princeton University and .... (become) a Commander of Arts and Letters in France. Many colleges .... (start) Dylan Studies course. He .... (make) three films and .... (travel) all over the world.

(c) Tropical reefs .... (exist) for more than 500 million years. Because lands that once lay in the tropics .... (drift) with time, ancient reefs are often found in regions that are temperate today. In more recent times, changes in sea level .... (affect) reefs. The sea .... (be) at its present level only in the past 5 000 years. 15 000 years ago the sea was 120 metres lower than it is today.

TASK TWO

Write down:

all the places you have visited or lived in
some of the books you have read
some of the films you have seen
some of the sports events you have watched
some of the games you have played
any other things you have done or learned in the past which you think have made a difference to your life now.

Then tell your partner about some of these things and ask your partner about her/his life.

For example:

I've been to Thailand but I can't speak Thai. Have you been to Thailand?
I've read John Updike's books and I'm going to read his new one. Have you read 'Rabbit at Rest'?
I've never seen the film 'Casablanca' so I'm going to rent a video. Have you seen 'Casablanca'?

Unit 2.22
USED TO
Form

She used to play tennis.
You used to study very hard.
It used to cost five pounds.

HOW TO FORM IT

Used to is followed by the *stem (infinitive)* form of the verb. Like all past forms, it is the same for all the pronoun or noun subjects:

Subject	Used to	Stem	Example
I You She/he It We They	used to	eat study play cost travel go	I used to eat a lot of chocolate. You used to study very hard. She used to play tennis. It used to cost five pounds. We used to travel by bus. They used to go to Cascaes every summer.

HOW TO FORM THE NEGATIVE

There are different ways of forming the *negative*. The most common way in British and American English is:

They *didn't used to* buy expensive books.

but

They *used not to* buy expensive books.
is also common.

Another way is to use *never* instead of *did + not*:

They *never used to* buy expensive clothes.

HOW TO FORM QUESTIONS

There is only one way to form a question using *used to:*

> *Did* you *use* (or *used*) *to* play basket-ball?
> *Did* she *use* (or *used*) *to* speak French?

But many people prefer not to use *used to* in questions and use a different way of asking the question:

> Did you play football when you were in school/when you were young?
> Did she speak French when she was a child?

The answer can be 'Yes' or 'No' but we usually add the pronoun and *did*:

> Did you use (or used) to play basket-ball?   Yes, *I did.*

You can also say 'I don't know'. If you add anything after 'I don't know', then you have to use '*if* + pronoun + *did*':

> Did she speak French when she was a child?   I don't know *if she did.*

WARNING BOX

'Used' in *used to* is pronounced /juːst/. The past form of the verb *use* is *used* and is pronounced /juːzd/.

Tasks to practise this form are included in the next unit.

I used to make a fortune writing short stories.
The sparling fish used to breed in the River Forth.
She used to work for the Post Office.

WHEN TO USE IT

We use *used to*:

(a) to talk about a habit, action or state in the past. It can only be used for *past* time. We usually only use *used to* about things that are no longer true at the time of speaking or writing:

'In the golden age of magazines in the Fifties,' said writer Kurt Vonnegut, 'I *used to* make a fortune writing short stories. But that was before television came along.'

The sparling fish has come back to the River Forth after being absent for 25 years. The fish *used to* breed in the river but it disappeared in 1965. Now environmentalists hope it will start breeding again.

It *used to* take 18 hours to fly from Rio de Janeiro to New York.

(b) to talk about something we did in the past that we no longer do. We can also use *used to* to talk about things that we believed to be true in the past but that we now no longer believe:

> She *used to* work for the Post Office in Scotland but two years ago she moved to England and started working for ICI.

> People *used to* think that the earth was like a flat cake with the sea all around it. But we know now that it's really like an orange – not quite round like a ball but a little flattened at the top and bottom like an orange.

Another way of talking about things that we did in the past is to use *would + stem*. This is more common in written English but we often start with *used to* and then use *would*. *Used to* is more common in spoken English, and *would* is more common in written English:

> When I was young I *used to* go to the cinema every Saturday afternoon. My friend Joyce lived farther away so she *would* phone me when she was leaving her house to catch the bus. I *would* wait ten minutes and then walk to the bus stop. Then I *would* wait for the bus Joyce was on so that I could join her. Once I was late and Joyce had to get off the bus and wait for me.

TASK ONE

You can do this task orally with a partner or you can write it down.

*Ellen Smith was born in 1962. When she was a child she did things that she doesn't do any more. Look at the following list of her ideas and activities and make some statements about her life when she was young and her life now. Use the pattern **used to + stem (infinitive)**.*

Ellen Smith: hobbies and interests

	1960s and 1970s	1990s
(a)	badminton	tennis
(b)	swimming	skiing
(c)	read historical novels	reads biographies
(d)	went to the cinema	watches videos
(e)	studied for exams	sets exams
(f)	spoke French	speaks English
(g)	collected stamps	doesn't collect anything
	Ideas and Plans	*Lifestyle*
(h)	wanted to be a business executive	is a university lecturer
(i)	planned to live in Belgium	lives in Canada
(j)	didn't like travelling	goes on many trips

For example:
Ellen Smith used to collect stamps but now she doesn't collect anything.

TASK TWO

Write down some of the things you used to do when you were young. Then tell a partner or write a short account of these things.

For example:
What did you used to:
    do in the school holidays?   read?
    think about school?   do for exercise?
    do for fun at weekends?   plan for the future?
What was your daily routine when you were young? How has your life changed? What did you use to do that you don't do now?

TASK THREE

*Tell or write a short story about something that you used to do. Begin with **used to** and then continue with **would**. (Look at the story about Joyce at the end of Unit 2.23 USED TO Function for an example.)*

133

Unit 2.24
PASSIVE
Form

'Sunflowers' was painted by Van Gogh.
5000 people are killed on the roads every year.
Andrew was given the prize.

Look at this sentence:

Van Gogh painted a picture of 'Sunflowers'.

In Unit 1.1 we looked at how sentences were made up:

Subject + Verb + Object

The sentence above is in the <u>active</u> form and is divided like this:

Subject	Verb	Object
Van Gogh	painted	a picture of 'Sunflowers'.

But we can say the same thing in another way, called the <u>passive</u>:

A picture of 'Sunflowers' was painted by Van Gogh.

Now we've turned things around:

Subject	Verb	Agent
A picture of 'Sunflowers'	was painted	by Van Gogh.

NOTES: The *subject* of the active sentence becomes the *agent*. To form the passive we use the verb *be* + the past participle of the main verb.

Sometimes there are two objects in an active sentence:

Subject	Verb	Indirect Object	Direct Object
They	will give	Andrew	the prize.

In this example we have a choice of subject and therefore two ways to form the *passive*:

Either:

Subject	Verb	Indirect Object
The prize	will be given	to Andrew.

or:

Subject	Verb	Direct Object
Andrew	will be given	the prize.

But, it isn't always necessary to have an agent. In the example above, the agent (who gave the prize to Andrew) is unimportant. In the following example, we don't know who the agent is:

Subject	Verb	Adverbials
Five thousand people	are killed	on the road every year.

TASK ONE

Rewrite the following sentences in the passive form. Decide where you will use an agent.

(a) Fred saw Raymond at the theatre.
(b) The storm destroyed many of the houses.
(c) They are going to sell cars in that showroom.
(d) Juliet held the horse's reins.
(e) They made a film of Mozart's life.
(f) Graham Greene wrote 'Brighton Rock'.
(g) The Prime Minister met the President in the Bahamas.
(h) The British ruled India for 200 years.
(i) They executed Fawkes for treason.
(j) The young visitors gave their grandmother flowers on her birthday.

TASK TWO

Make up passive sentences suggested by these pictures.

Unit 2.25
PASSIVE
Function

Penicillin was discovered by Fleming.
Five goals were scored.
Marriages are made in Heaven.

HOW TO USE IT

We use the *passive*:

(a) to focus on what we are talking about. We can say
either:

> Fleming discovered penicillin.

or

> Penicillin was discovered by Fleming.

We would choose the first example if we are talking about Fleming and the second if
we are talking about penicillin.

(b) to focus on the action and not the person:

> Five goals were scored.

Here we are not interested in who scored the goals, but in the fact that five goals were
scored.

(c) when we don't know the agent:

> Marriages are made in Heaven.

Here we can't name somebody who makes marriages.

TASK ONE

Make up sentences so that the word or phrase underlined is the focus. The sentences can be active or passive. You must have the right tense.

For example:
> Cervantes – write – 'Don Quixote'.
> *'Don Quixote' was written by Cervantes.*

(a) Barth – write – 'Sot-weed Factor'.
(b) Prayers – say – the teacher.
(c) House – paint – the old man.
(d) The window – break – the little girl.
(e) Chairs – make – Gillow
(f) Walt Disney – create – Mickey Mouse.
(g) Frank – give – the weather forecast.
(h) Juliet – love – Romeo.
(i) The Queen – meet – the captain.
(j) Margaret – elect – the people.

TASK TWO

Rewrite this short paragraph, so that the words underlined become the focus.

Philip wrote the book early in 1989. The public liked it and it became a bestseller. His publishers asked Philip to write a sequel. They would publish the sequel a year later. All this frightened Philip. He didn't think he could work that fast and he had no ideas. But his wife thought it was a good idea. She encouraged him to sign the contract.

For example:
> The book was written by Philip early in 1989.

After a few winters you will get used to the cold weather in Canada.
He isn't used to cooking his own meals.

HOW TO FORM IT

There is another meaning of *used to* when it is used with the verb *be* or *get* and is followed by:

either a noun phrase:
   get used to **the weather**
   be used to **the food**

or by the *-ing* form of the verb:
   be used to **cooking**
   get used to **living** in a small house

Used to has only one form and so it doesn't change, whether you are talking about the present, the past or the future. It is the verb *get* or *be* that changes:

You will soon *get used to* living here.	(future)
He *is used to eating* his main meal at noon.	(present form for a fact)
He *got used to* wearing a lot of clothes in winter.	(past time)
She's *getting used* to the accent in Glasgow.	(present continuous)
They *were* just *getting used to* Indian food when they moved to Japan.	(past continuous)
She's *been used to* working hard but now she has retired and has to find something to do with her time.	(present perfect)

WARNING BOX

'Used' in *used to* is pronounced /ju:st/. See the Warning Box in Unit 2.22.

WHEN TO USE IT

Get used to

To *get used to* something or someone means that you are becoming familiar with the person or thing and you no longer find them strange or unusual:

Now that she is living in Thailand she *is getting used to* eating rice every day.

You'll have to *get used to* doing the housework.

Be used to

To *be used to* someone or something means that you are familiar with it because you have seen or done it often or because you know someone well and are not surprised by their behaviour:

Tom *isn't used to* living on his own and is very lonely when his wife is away on business trips.

I know he can be very annoying but I*'m used to* him now so I don't notice.

When she first came to Lancaster she found it difficult to understand people in the shops but now she *is used to* the way they speak.

COMMON EXPRESSIONS

getting used to it

becoming accustomed to something.

A. How are you?

B. I'm okay. The weather is very cold but I*'m getting used to it.*

140

TASK ONE

After many years away from school, you have decided to join an English class. At first you found it very strange and difficult to be a student again. You are now starting to find it easier. How would you answer someone who asks you how you are getting on as a student?

Think of all the things you are getting used to doing: sitting in class, studying, making mistakes, doing homework, etc.

For example:
> At first I found everything very strange but now I'm getting used to things.

TASK TWO

1. *Some people have come to live in your city from another country. They find some of the things about your way of life different and they have to learn to do things your way. You want to tell them that after a while they will become familiar with all the strange things. Think of some of the things that English or American people might find different in your country. Work with a partner orally or write down the things you could tell them. Use 'You'll get used to . . .'*

   For example:
   > You'll get used to eating dinner at 9.30 at night.

2. *Now think of the things that people might have said they were not used to doing or seeing.*

   With a partner write these things down and exchange your list with another pair. Then make replies to what the people have said.

   For example:
   > I'm not used to eating rice every day.
   > You'll soon get used to it and then you won't want to eat potatoes.

```
┌─────────────────────────────────┐
│                                 │
│          Unit 2.27              │
│        MODAL VERBS              │
│           Form                  │
│                                 │
└─────────────────────────────────┘
```

You will find us next to the Superdrive.
Could you help me?
You needn't tell him.
He isn't able to do it this week.

HOW TO FORM SENTENCES

Because of the way modal verbs are used in sentences, we can divide them into three types: **Central**, **Marginal** and **Semi-auxiliary**. The table below shows you which modals belong to the different types.

Central modals	Marginal modals	Semi-auxiliaries
can could may might must ought to should will would	need	be able to have to

Central modals

These modal verbs have these characteristics:

(i) They are always followed by another verb without *to*:
Medical costs *can be* expensive.
You *might be* late.

(ii) You make the negative by putting *not* after the modal:
Visitors *must not [mustn't]* approach the animals.
He *won't find* it that easily.

142

(iii) You make questions by inverting the subject and modal:
       Could you help me?
       May I close the window?

(iv) You can't put two central modal verbs together:
       * You *must can* do it. (not possible)

(v) There are no tense forms.

(vi) There are no other forms, e.g., *+ing*, *+ed*.

NOTE: **There are no tense forms with central modals. Sometimes *could* or *was able to* is used as the past form of *can* (see Unit 2.29). *Had to* is used as a past reference for *must*.**

WARNING BOX

Didn't have to is *not* a past reference for *mustn't* (see Unit 2.28).

Marginal modals

These are modal verbs which can be used either like central modals or like main verbs:
       You *need*n't *tell* him. (central modal)
       Need I *go* there? (central modal)

       You don't need to tell him. (main verb)
       Do I need to go there? (main verb)

NOTE: ***Need* is also a main verb, as in *I need some money.***

Semi-auxiliaries

(i) These verbs are used like main verbs:
       He *isn't able to* do it this week. (negative)
       Will he *be able to* do it next week? (question)
       He *had to* see her. (past)
       They *didn't have to* go there. (past)
       I'll *have to* do it tonight. (future)

(ii) They can be used with another modal verb:
       You *must be able to* do it. (must + be able to)
       They *should be able to* help you. (should + be able to)

TASK ONE

In the following sentences identify the type of modal verb, by putting (a), (b), etc. in the appropriate column in the table below.

(a) Can you help me?
(b) I need to see the doctor.
(c) They couldn't get a ticket.
(d) She had to be there before 9.00.
(e) Must you do that?
(f) The car won't go.
(g) You shouldn't get angry with him.
(h) They're able to offer us 10 per cent discount.
(i) You ought to try to see him.
(j) Wouldn't it be lovely!

Central	Marginal	Semi-auxiliary

TASK TWO

How many sentences can you make from the following words? Each sentence must contain a modal verb.

you they hotel will can no-one me from thirty take can't is take enjoy everything help him away now of able to this us the there a way needn't do we work be house tonight must has lock at wouldn't doors go couldn't question night see understand wouldn't she

Unit 2.28
MODALS:
MUST/MUSTN'T
HAVE TO/DON'T HAVE TO
NEED/NEEDN'T/DON'T
NEED TO
Function

You must eat to live.
We'll have to get a visa.
British people need not obtain a visa to go to France.

WHEN TO USE THEM

(a) to talk about things it is important to do, or because it is a rule or legal obligation:

MUST and HAVE TO
You *must eat* to live.
Dogs *must be* kept on a leash.
In Australia, everyone aged eighteen or over *has to vote*.
Our parents *had to learn* things parrot-fashion.
A teacher *must* have a good sense of humour.

145

NOTES: With this use, we use *had to* to refer to the past. We also use the imperative form (see Units 1.4 and 1.5) to express obligation:
'Keep off the grass' means 'You must keep off the grass!'.

(b) to talk about things it is important for people not to do

MUST NOT [MUSTN'T]
On the motorway, you *mustn't* reverse or turn in the road.
Teachers in Europe *must not* hit their pupils.

NOTES: *Have to* does not express this use of *must*, but we also use *cannot* or *may not* (see Unit 2.29 and Unit 2.30) for *must not*:
You *can't/may not* reverse on the motorway.

When we want to refer to the past, we use *couldn't* (see Unit 2.29):
The land belonged to the army and you *couldn't* go near it.

The negative imperative can also be used (see Unit 1.5):
You *mustn't* make any noise.
Don't make any noise!

(c) when it is necessary to do something:

NEED and HAVE TO
British people *have to* get a visa to go to India.
I *need to* go out and enjoy myself.
This car *needs to* be serviced after every 10 000 miles.

(d) to talk about things which it is not necessary for people to do:

NEED NOT [NEEDN'T] and DON'T HAVE TO
British people *don't need to* obtain a visa to go to France.
You *needn't* worry about us.
You *don't have to* be a millionaire to buy a Picasso – but it helps.

WARNING BOX

The negative form *don't have to* is never used as an alternative form for *mustn't*. It is the alternative form for *needn't*.

(e) when we are certain about something, although we may not know exactly:

MUST

It *must* be lunchtime by now!
You *must* be Eric's son – you look just like him!

COMMON EXPRESSIONS

You must be joking.	When someone says something that you find difficult to believe.
Must you?	When you are irritated by what someone has said or done.
It's a must.	Telling someone that it is important for them to do it.
Needs must!	You will do anything, even if it is wrong, if it is very important.
Need I say more?	When you feel it is not necessary to give any further explanation.

147

TASK ONE

Read the following sentences and identify the meaning of the modal verb in each case by putting (a), (b), etc. in the appropriate place in the box.

(a) You must be there by two o'clock or they'll close the gates.
(b) You don't have to read every page.
(c) There were crowds of people at the demonstration. There must have been at least five thousand there.
(d) There must be six people present before we start. The rule says so.
(e) You need to prepare the dish three days before you eat it.
(f) Film stars always have to look glamorous.
(g) You mustn't stay out after ten.
(h) He had to see her.
(i) You didn't have to tell him.
(j) Now the family had got bigger, they needed a larger house.

IMPORTANT TO DO	
IMPORTANT NOT TO DO	
NECESSARY TO DO	
NOT NECESSARY TO DO	
CERTAIN ABOUT SOMETHING	

TASK TWO

*Here are some notes from Peter's diary. Read them through and make a list of the things Peter **must do**, **needs to do**, **mustn't do**, etc.*

October 4th: go to bank – arrange a loan
haven't got any biscuits – buy some
don't water the plants – too much water kills them
Mary's birthday – don't forget theatre tickets

October 10th: important: take car to garage for service
send Robert the money owed
don't tell Jane about holiday with Mary
kitchen light broken – buy new fixture

TASK THREE

What would you say in the following situations? Use the common expressions explained in this Unit.

(a) There was something you had to do, although you knew it might be illegal.
(b) A friend tells you that your boss has been arrested for not paying his train fares. You find this difficult to believe.
(c) A colleague has been telling people how to organise their business, although he had been unsuccessful as a manager.

149

Unit 2.29
MODALS:
CAN, COULD
Function

You can take a horse to water, but you can't make it drink.
I can't find the English papers anywhere.
You could be speaking another language in twelve weeks' time.
Could you come to dinner next week?

WHEN TO USE THEM

We use *can* and *could*:

(a) to tell us if someone is able to (or not able to) do something:
  You *can* take a horse to water but you *can't* make it drink.
  Lee *can* drive now.
  Marc has grown a lot. He *can* touch the ceiling in his room.

NOTE: *Be able to* is used to talk about the future:
  He'll *be able to* reach the top shelf soon. See Unit 2.30 (a).

150

(b) to tell us what we are allowed to do (or not allowed to do):
>   That land belongs to the university but you *can* walk across it.
>   That land belonged to the President, and you *couldn't* go in there.

NOTE: *Could* is the past form of *can* when we are talking about what someone was *able to do* or what they were *allowed to do*:
>   A few years ago you *could* buy it for half that price.
>   I *couldn't* get in because I was too young.

With the following uses, *can* and *could* have similar meanings. *Could* never refers to the past.

(c) to tell us if something is possible:
>   We *can* buy it all at Supersave.
>   You *could* be speaking another language in twelve weeks' time.

NOTE: See (a) above and Unit 2.30(a).

(d) to make suggestions about what to do:
>   You *can* always phone me if you have a problem.
>   The film finishes early, so we *could* eat afterwards.

NOTE: In (c) and (d), *could* is usual, although *can* is possible.

(e) to ask permission (or refuse permission):
>   *Can* Hannah come out to play?
>   No, she *can't*.
>   *Can* I stay up late to watch the film?
>   *Could* I stay up late to watch the film?
>   *Couldn't* I stay up to watch the film?

(f) to invite people (meaning 'Is it possible?' but being polite):
>   We've got an extra ticket – *can* you join us?
>   *Could* you come to dinner next week?
>   *Couldn't* you come to dinner next week?

NOTE: In (e) and (f), the use of the negative form *couldn't* makes asking permission or inviting much stronger.

(g) to make a request:
>   I'm very busy now. *Can* you do it?
>   I'm very busy now. *Could* you do it?
>   I'm very busy now. *Can't* you do it?
>   I'm very busy now. *Couldn't* you do it?

NOTE: The use of the negative form *can't* or *couldn't* makes the request stronger.

151

(h) to show we are almost certain about something:
    A: Who's that?
    B: It *could* be John. He often comes at this time.

COMMON EXPRESSIONS

You can't be serious!   You say this to someone when they tell you something that you don't believe.

I couldn't say.   You say this when you don't know the answer to something.

Could be.   You say this when something is possible, but you're not certain and you're not very interested.

TASK ONE

This picture shows the house where an old woman lived. What suggestions do you have for getting rid of the things left in the house after she died?

For example:

We could sell this to a secondhand shop.
We could give these to charity.

TASK TWO

*Using **can** or **could**, decide what the people are saying in the pictures.*

For example: Picture (a)
   Could you come to dinner next week?

(a)

(b)

(c)

(d)

(e)

(f)

TASK THREE

Visitors have come to your home town. Tell them what they can or could do there.

For example:
   There's a good local museum, you could visit that.
   The sports centre is very good. You can play squash there.

TASK FOUR

What would you say in the following situations? Use the common expressions that are explained in this Unit.

(a) A neighbour asks you if it is true that the new neighbour is very rich. You don't know and you aren't interested.
(b) A friend tells you she is planning to spend a holiday climbing in the Alps. You know she doesn't like heights.
(c) A friend asks you if your sister is going to be at home tonight. You don't know.

Unit 2.30
MODALS:
MAY/MAY NOT,
MIGHT/MIGHT NOT
Function

It may rain tomorrow.
Might I stay for three nights?
May I go out tonight?
You may not park here.

WHEN TO USE THEM

We use *may* and *might*:

(a) to talk about a possible future event:
It *may* rain tomorrow.
They *might* not like it.

NOTE: *Could* **is also used in this meaning (see Unit 2.29 (a) and (c)):**
It *could* rain tomorrow.
Generally *may* suggests that the event is the most probable, then *might*, then *could*
(the least likely):

MAY ——————— MIGHT ——————— COULD		
probable ←——————— possible ———————→ unlikely		

(b) to make polite requests:
May I use your phone?
Might I stay for three nights?

NOTES: *Can* **and *could* are also used for requests (see Unit 2.29(g)). *Might* is very polite**
but is not used very often. *May* and *could* are the most usual. *Can* is often used
but is considered to be less polite.

(a) to give permission:
A: May I go out tonight?
B: Yes, you *may*.

156

NOTES: *Might* is not possible with this meaning. *Can* is possible, but it is very direct and sometimes less polite.

(d) to refuse permission:
    A: May I go out tonight?
    B: No, you *may not.*

NOTES: *Cannot/can't* is also used (see Unit 2.9(e)). *Mayn't* is very unusual and never used to end a statement.

(e) to tell us of a prohibition or restriction:
    You *may* only park in the space shown.
    You *may not* park on the carriageway itself.

NOTE: *Mustn't* and *can't* are also used (see Units 2.28 and 2.29).

COMMON EXPRESSIONS

Maybe.   When something is possible, but you are not very interested.

I might have known. } When you are disappointed or irritated about something that
I might have guessed. } has happened.

TASK ONE

*Below there are lots of uses of **may** and **might**. Underline each one and state what meaning each one has.*

(a) 'We may go to New York for our holidays,' John always said to people who asked him about holidays. 'But, we may not.' People were always confused.

(b)

(c)

TASK TWO

*Look at TASK ONE again and replace **may** and **might** with other forms, such as **can** and **could**, wherever possible.*

TASK THREE

What would you say in the following situations? Use the common expressions that are explained in this Unit.

(a) You had planned to go to a theatre with a friend. The friend telephones at the last minute to say he can't come because he has to do some important work. You are very disappointed.

(b) Someone asks if it is true that a famous actor will be visiting the town. It is probably true, but you are not interested.

158

Unit 2.31
MODALS:
SHOULD/SHOULD NOT
OUGHT TO/OUGHT
NOT TO
Function

You should use the paths in the countryside.
Schools ought to have more games and sports.
You should see the doctor.
It ought to be very hot in July.

WHEN TO USE THEM

(a) to talk about things it is important to do, but which we can't make people do:
You *should* use the paths in the countryside. Don't walk across the fields.
You *shouldn't* throw away lighted cigarettes.
Oughtn't he *to* apologise?

NOTE: With this meaning, *ought not to* is not common except in questions. Use *should not.*

(b) to talk about what it is better to do or to have:
There *should* be smaller classes.
Teachers *should* get more money.
Schools *ought to* have more sports.

(c) to give advice or give an opinion:
You *should* see the doctor.
You *ought to* get the early train.

(d) to talk about something which is probable or which we are almost certain will happen:
The train arrives at 12.29, so Tony *should* be here by one o'clock.
The book *should* be on the desk by the window.

NOTE: In all these examples, it is possible to use *ought to.*

COMMON EXPRESSIONS

Why should I?	When you don't want to do something, and want to show the person who asked you that you are angry at being asked.
How should I know?	When you don't know something and are angry at being asked.

160

TASK ONE

*In the following sentences, identify the meaning of **should** or **ought to**, by putting the sentence number in the appropriate place in the box below.*

(a) They ought to try a different bank.
(b) You should say you're sorry.
(c) There ought to be bigger fines for drunken driving.
(d) He leaves work at 5.00, so he should be here by 7.00.
(e) You ought to water your plants.
(f) There shouldn't be any difficulty arranging the appointment.
(g) You shouldn't leave bits of broken glass around.
(h) You should have warned me you would be late.
(i) You should lose weight and exercise more.
(j) It ought to be hot and sunny in August.

IMPORTANT TO DO	
BETTER TO DO OR TO HAVE	
GIVE ADVICE OR AN OPINION	
ALMOST CERTAIN	

TASK TWO

Look at the pictures below and decide what advice you would give.

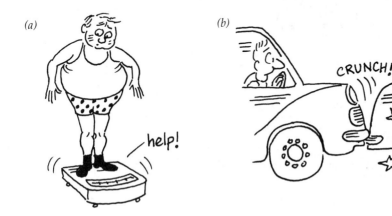

(a)

(b)

help!

CRUNCH!

(c)

(d)

(e)

TASK THREE

Respond to these requests and show you are angry at being asked. Use the common expressions that are explained in this Unit.

(a) What's the name of the Argentinian writer who lived in Paris and wrote 'Hopscotch'?

(b) Could you check these papers? Mr Alban's on leave.

162

It'll rain tomorrow.
Will you have a holiday this year?
Shall we dance?
Dishwashers won't wash clothes.

WHEN TO USE THEM

We use *will, will not [won't]* and *shall, shall not [shan't]*:

(a) to predict something about the future:
    It'*ll* rain tomorrow.
    I'*ll* miss you.

(b) to ask about the future:
    Will you have a holiday this year?
    Will you get the tickets?
    How *shall* I know which house is yours?

NOTE: *Will* and *shall* in (a) and (b) relate to the future (see Unit 2.15).

WARNING BOX

In the second example in (b), the speaker is asking if the other person will get the tickets. This is a simple enquiry. Compare this with the first example in (c), where the speaker is suggesting that he/she should get the tickets.

(c) to make suggestions when we want to or are willing to do something:
    Shall I get the tickets?
    Shall we dance?

NOTES: *Will* is not possible with this meaning. *Shall* is used only with *I* or *we* and most often with *we*. An alternative form is '*Let's*..', e.g. '*Let's go to the cinema*'.

163

(d) to ask someone to do something:
     Will you help me move my office?
     Will you come with me to the party?

NOTES: *Could* is more often used here (see Unit 2.29). *Would* is also used when we want to be very polite (see Unit 2.33).

(e) to talk about something that is generally true:
     If you drop it, it *will* break.
     Dishwashers *won't* wash clothes.

NOTE: *Shall* is not possible with (d) and (e).

COMMON EXPRESSIONS

These things will happen! ⎱ When you feel that something is inevitable, usually
These things happen!   ⎰ something unpleasant or unfortunate.

TASK ONE

*Identify the meanings of **will** and **shall** in the sentences below, by putting the number of the sentence in the appropriate place in the table below.*

(a) Oil won't mix with water.
(b) You'll need a lot of money soon.
(c) Will you take Gareth to the cinema, please?
(d) Shall we go out to eat tonight?
(e) Shall we learn Russian this year?
(f) Will you learn Russian this year?
(g) You won't like that film. It's very violent.
(h) Will you do the washing-up, please?
(i) It'll be much colder if it rains.
(j) Will you go if it's raining?

GENERAL TRUTH	
ASKING ABOUT THE FUTURE	
PREDICTION	
REQUEST	
SUGGESTION	

TASK TWO

Make a list of five people you know, and then make notes predicting what they will do or what will happen to them this year.

For example:
    John will get married.
    Mary will be successful in her job.

TASK THREE

A friend is visiting your home town. You want to go out tonight. Make suggestions about what you could do.

For example:
    Shall we go for a walk by the river?

Would you give me a lift home?
Would you mind if I opened the window?

WHEN TO USE IT

We use *would*[*'d*], *would not* [*wouldn't*]:

(a) to ask someone to do something when we want to be polite:

(i) WOULD
Would you lend me your copy of 'Don Quixote'?
Would you give me a lift home? My car's at the garage.

NOTE: *Could* is often used instead of *would* here. So are *will* and *can* but these are less polite. The best answer is 'Yes, of course'.

(ii) WOULD YOU MIND
Would you mind lending me your copy of 'Don Quixote'?
Would you mind giving me a lift home?

NOTES: The polite response here is 'No, of course not'. *Would you mind . . . ?* can also be used to express annoyance, e.g. *'Would you mind stopping that noise!'* or *'Would you mind closing the door!'* In these examples you are showing that the noise disturbs you or that you don't like the door open.

(b) to ask permission when we want to be very polite:
Would you mind if I opened the window?
Would you mind if Jane came with us?

NOTE: Again the polite response is 'No, of course not'.

(c) to make a polite suggestion or offer:
Would you like me to open the window?

(d) to show that we are annoyed:
She *would* refuse – she always does!
You *wouldn't* dare!

166

COMMON EXPRESSIONS

You would, wouldn't you!   Telling someone that what they have done is typical of them.

Would I do that?   } Showing surprise that you have been accused of doing
Would I do such a thing?   } something.

TASK ONE

How would you ask for something in the following situations?

(a) You need some money to buy some food.
(b) Some children are playing outside and you want to work.
(c) Your car's broken down.
(d) You want the radio switched off.
(e) You want to bring a friend to a party with you.
(f) You want to go home early from work.
(g) You want your friend to look after your children until seven o'clock.
(h) You are going to be late. You ask a friend to tell another friend, George, to wait for you.
(i) You are busy and your telephone rings. You ask your friend to answer it.
(j) You want your friend to make some tea.

TASK TWO

In the situations illustrated below, one person is requesting something or asking for permission. What do you think they are saying? Give the response.

For example: Picture (a):
    A: Would you help me put up this tent?
    B: Certainly./Yes, of course.

(a)   *(b)*

(c)   *(d)*

(e)

If it's cheap, people will buy it.
If you take the back road, there's very little traffic.
If it were cheap, people would buy it.

HOW TO FORM IT

We can form this conditional in three ways:

Type A

If part	Main part
If + present	modal (usually *will*) + main verb (stem without *to*)

If it's cheap,   people will buy it.

Type B

If part	Main part
If + present	main verb present

If you take the back road,   there's very little traffic.

Type C

If part	Main part
If + past	modal (usually *would*) + main verb (stem without *to*)

If it were cheap,   people would buy it.

169

NOTES: The two parts of the sentence can be reversed:
People will buy it if it's cheap.
There's very little traffic if you take the back road.
People would buy it if it were cheap.

For Types A and B, we can use the *imperative* form (see Units 1.4 and 1.5) instead of the *if* part of the sentence. Then we connect the two parts of the sentence with *and*:
Take the back road and there's very little traffic.

TASK ONE

Match the part of the sentence on the left with an appropriate part from the right.

(a)	If you see the bear,	he won't be here until after midnight.
(b)	If you come home late,	they'll buy it.
(c)	If the house fell down,	you'll be successful.
(d)	If you see him coming,	you'll find a lot of bargains.
(e)	If you saw him in the morning,	he would worry.
(f)	If the train was late,	she would always be angry.
(g)	If she was ill,	you must tell mother.
(h)	If you go early,	we'd be all right.
(i)	If the exam is easy,	there'll be no food left.
(j)	If they like it,	you mustn't be afraid.

TASK TWO

Look at the sentences you have made in TASK ONE.

(a) *Use the following table to write down what type they are:*

Type A	Type B	Type C

(b) *Write alternative forms (imperatives) where it is possible.*

For example:
   Come home late and there'll be no food left.

171

If it rains tomorrow, they'll stop the carnival.
If she hears his name, she becomes angry.

WHEN TO USE IT

We use this conditional:

(a) to describe or state a habit (Type B):
   If she hears his name, she becomes very angry.
   If it was a bright morning, he always walked to work.

NOTE: *If* can be replaced by *whenever, when* or *each time that* . . .:
   Each time she hears his name, she becomes very angry.
   Whenever it was a bright morning, he always walked to work.

(b) to express future certainties (Type A):
   If you get the answer to the second problem, you'll win the prize.
   If it rains tomorrow, they'll stop the carnival.
   If the train's on time here, then it should be on time at Crewe.

NOTE: Here the focus is on the main part of the sentence. The situation or event is certain or likely if the possibility expressed in the *if* part happens.

(c) to express future possibilities (Type C):
   If it rained tomorrow, they'd stop the carnival.
   If you sent her a card, she'd be very happy.

NOTE: This is very similar to (b) but the focus is on the *if* part of the sentence. The speaker doesn't expect the possibility expressed in the *if* part to happen.

(d) to express advice (Type A):
   If you lose your way, phone us.
   If you're selling your house, come and see us.

172

(e) to make a suggestion (Type A):

> If you come on Saturday, we can go for a walk on Sunday.
> If you take the back road, there'll be very little traffic.

NOTE: You can also use the past tense to make the suggestion:
If you came on Saturday, we could go for a walk on Sunday.

(f) to state a fact (Type B):

> If you take the back road, there's very little traffic.
> If you heat metal, it expands.

NOTE: With (e) and (f), it is possible to use the imperative form (see Unit 1.5):
> Come on Saturday, and we can go for a walk on Sunday.
> Take the back road, and there'll be very little traffic.
> Take the back road, and there's very little traffic.
> Heat metal and it expands.

COMMON EXPRESSIONS

If the cap fits, wear it.	You are suggesting that a previous comment applies to the person addressed.
To be iffy.	To show you are uncertain about something. A. 'Are you going to Barcelona for your holiday?' B. 'It's a bit *iffy* yet.'
Ifs and buts.	When you are expressing doubts about whether something is going to happen. A. 'Will they build the new factory here?' B. 'I don't know, it's full of *ifs and buts*.'

173

TASK ONE

In each of the sentences below, identify the type of possible condition used and write the number of the sentence in the appropriate place in the table below.

(a) If the car's all right, we'll go away for the weekend.
(b) If she woke up early in the morning, she would go for a run before work.
(c) If you're in a hurry, phone us for a taxi.
(d) If you go to the park on Sundays, there's always a band playing.
(e) If you find the ring, give it to the hotel manager.
(f) If you win the first round, you'll probably do well in the rest of the competition.
(g) If you find that book boring, you won't enjoy any of the others.
(h) If she came back tomorrow, we'd be able to start the work.
(i) If the bus is late, we'll miss the beginning of the film.
(j) If I win the money this week, I'll leave my job and start a new life.

Habit	
Future certainties	
Future possibilities	
Advice	
Suggestions	
Facts	

TASK TWO

*Here is the beginning of a story about a man who might win some money and what he will do. Read it and then continue in the same way, adding an **if** sentence each time. (If you do it with some friends, go round the group with each person adding a sentence.)*

> If John wins the race, he'll get £100.
> If he gets £100, he'll go out with his friends.
> If he goes out with his friends...

Now you continue.

TASK THREE

How would you respond to what these people say? Use the common expressions that are explained in this Unit.

(a) *Jane:* Do you think they'll decide to change the directors?
   You: ...
(b) *Jim:* If you're suggesting that I was responsible for losing that money...
   You: Not at all, but...

174

CONDITIONAL: IMPOSSIBLE
Form

If you had £10, you could go.
If he were here, he would explain it.

HOW TO FORM IT

If part	Main part
If + past simple	past modal + main verb (stem without *to*)

If you had £10,   you could go.
If he were here,   he would explain it.

WARNING BOX

With the past form of the verb *be*, *were* is usually used instead of *was*, especially following *I*, *he* and *she*:

TASK ONE

Complete the following sentences.

(a) If John .... (be) in Venice, he could see the carnival now.
(b) If it .... (rain), we .... (go) to the cinema.
(c) If you .... (have) a video, you could record the film.
(d) If Anna hadn't got married, she .... (enter) for the Miss World competition.
(e) If Sammy .... (go) to the gym regularly, he would have won the Mr Hot Bod competition.
(f) If you .... (have) an invitation, you could go to the party.
(g) If you .... (drive), we could hire a car for the holiday.
(h) If you were younger, you .... (enjoy) rock music.
(i) If Mavis .... (be) rich, she would travel by Concorde.
(j) If it was a funny film, I .... (go and see) it.

TASK TWO

Match the clauses on the left with the appropriate clauses on the right.

(a)	If I was a rich man,	you wouldn't go.
(b)	If Japan were nearer,	she'd forgive you.
(c)	If you read 'The Times',	she'd be a big star.
(d)	If pigs could fly,	he'd make a great film.
(e)	If the wind blew strongly,	they would look very funny.
(f)	If I crashed his car,	the windows would break.
(g)	If he had millions of dollars,	my dad would be very angry.
(h)	If she had talent,	you'd be better informed.
(i)	If she really loved you,	I'd go there more often.
(j)	If you thought about it,	I'd help the poor.

Compare your sentences with a colleague.

176

Unit 2.37
CONDITIONAL: IMPOSSIBLE
Function

If I had a camera, I would be able to take pictures.
If he were taller, he could post the letter.

WHEN TO USE IT

We use this conditional when the situation in the *if* part is impossible *now*:

IF I HAD A CAMERA I WOULD BE ABLE TO TAKE A LOVELY PICTURE

(but he hasn't, so he can't).

IF THE PRIEST WERE HERE HE WOULD EXPLAIN IT...

(but he isn't here, so nobody can explain it).

OMNEM CREDE DIEM TIBI DILUXISSE SUPREMUM

IF I WERE TALLER I COULD POST THE LETTER

(but he isn't, so he can't).

177

TASK ONE

Look at the people in this picture, then write down what you think they would like to do. Use
If. . ., he/she . . . .

For example:

    If she had her paints with her, she would paint it.

TASK TWO

Write down what you would do or you could see if you went to these places.

For example: London
You: If I went to London, I would visit the Houses of Parliament.

(a) Paris
(b) Peking
(c) Sidney
(d) New York
(e) Rio de Janeiro
(f) Bombay

(g) Tehran
(h) Mexico City
(i) The Antarctic
(j) The North Pole
(k) A desert island

TASK THREE

Ask five people you know what they would like to do or like to be and find out why they can't do those things or be that person. Then write down comments like these:

For example:

    Daisy would like to live in New York, but she has no money.
    If Daisy was rich, she would live in New York.

    Jimmy would like to be Fred Astaire, but he can't dance.
    If Jimmy could dance, he would be a film star.

178

Unit 2.38
CONDITIONAL: WISHING
Form and function

I wish I were a rich man.
He wishes the government would cut taxes.
They wish they lived in the country.
If only they would go away.

HOW TO FORM IT

There are two ways to express wishes:

(a) using *wish*:

> I wish I were a rich man.
> He wishes the government would cut taxes.
> They wish they lived in the country.

The important thing to notice is that the second part of the sentence – the wish – is put in the past tense:

I wish (present simple)	I were (past simple)...
They wish (present simple)	they lived (past simple)...

The general structure is similar to that for indirect statements (see Unit 2.39).

(b) using *if only*:

> If only I were rich.
> If only they would go away.

NOTE: **When we are speaking in the first person, e.g.** *I wish*, **it is possible to use** *if only* **instead of** *I wish*:

> **I wish I were rich.**   **If only I were rich.**
> **I wish he would phone. If only he would phone.**

179

WARNING BOX

After *I wish* or *If only*, we often say *I were* or *he were* instead of *was*, because we are wishing for something impossible.

WHEN TO USE THEM

We use the verb *wish* generally, when we want things to be different.

We use *if only* when we are irritated by the circumstances or regret the situation. (See the Note in (b)).

TASK ONE

*Here are some things people **would like** to do or **would like** to happen. Rewrite them as wishes.*

For example:

   I'd like to go to the moon and look down at the earth.
   Answer: I wish I could go to the moon and look down at the earth.
   I'd like them to stop that awful noise.
   Answer: If only they'd stop that awful noise.

(a) He'd like to travel round the world in a yacht.
(b) She'd like the disco near her house to close.
(c) They'd like to have a very big house in the country.
(d) She'd like it to rain on Sunday.
(e) He'd like to spend all his time in a library reading and studying.
(f) I'd like to be a famous dancer.
(g) He'd like to ride a horse like a cowboy.
(h) She'd like to run a big company.
(i) He'd like to live his schooldays again and work harder.
(j) I'd like to fly like a bird.

TASK TWO

What are these people wishing now?

TASK THREE

Ask some people you know what they would wish for if they had three wishes. Then write a report.

For example:

   Dennis wished that (a) he could retire soon; (b) he lived by the sea; (c) he was a good sailor.

The Prime Minister says inflation is the priority.

Joe says he's coming home next week.

He told us he was going to be absent.

In the first example, the newspaper is reporting what the Prime Minister has said:

Major says (that) inflation is the priority.

The subject of the statement does not refer to the person who is speaking.

RULE: To report what someone has said, use:

say + the statement.

NOTE: It is possible to put *that* after *say*, but it is not used very often.

In the second example, Joe's mother is telling his father what Joe said in a postcard:

He says (that) he's coming home next week.

Because the person referred to (Joe) is not the same as the person speaking, we change *I* to *he*:

'I'm coming home next week.'

Joe says (that) he's coming home next week.

In this example, the speaker is talking about something in the past, so we change the verb to the past:

'I'm going to be absent.'
Robert told us he *was going to be absent*.

RULE: When we are talking about the past, we change the present to the past form.

NOTES: It is also possible to use the verb *say* here:
He said he was going to be absent.

It is also possible to use the present form after *said*. We do this when the event has not happened yet:
He said he's going to be absent.

When we use the verb *tell*, we must also use a direct object:
He told *us* he was going to be absent.

TASK ONE

Mary Roberts, a well-known writer, has disappeared. A lot of people are talking about what might have happened to her. Look at the picture and report what the people are saying.

(a) *Bob Bruce*: 'I saw her driving to Bristol on Wednesday.'
(b) *Donna Wallace*: 'She's gone to see her mother in Australia.'
(c) *Joe Burgess*: 'She's getting married again.'
(d) *Daisy Runcorn*: 'Her first husband has come back.'
(e) *Phil Read*: 'I never liked her. She's gone and I'm glad.'
(f) *Rita Golding*: 'She's had an accident.'
(g) *Norman Enright*: 'She's in hospital near Chelmsford.'
(h) *Ed Young*: 'She's bought a mansion in Switzerland.'
(i) *Al Reynolds*: 'The tax people wanted her.'
(j) *Maggy May*: 'Her son is ill.'

TASK TWO

Anne has a problem. She came to work on her bicycle. Now she has bought some groceries and has to collect some clothes from the dry cleaners. How can she get everything home?

(a) *If you are doing this task at home, write down all your ideas. Then give your ideas to a friend. The friend then writes a report of your ideas.*

For example:
    She suggests that Anne should ask a friend to look after her bicycle and take the bus home.

(b) *If you are in a class, divide into groups. Each group tries to find a solution. One person from group one goes to group two and quietly tells them the group one solution. Group two then reports group one's solution to group three.*

This procedure is followed by each group, so that all the groups have to make a report on another group's suggestions.

When all the groups have heard all the suggestions, they must decide which solution is best.

184

Unit 2.40
INDIRECT SPEECH: QUESTIONS, REQUESTS, IMPERATIVES
Form

He asked him if there was going to be an election.
They asked him when there was going to be an election.
He asked him to call an election.

The Prime Minister is asked two questions in the picture above.

(a) a *yes/no* question:
   'Is there going to be an election?'

When talking about the reporter who asked a question, we can say:
   He asked the Prime Minister *if* there was going to be an election.

185

RULES: (i) To report a question, use the verb *ask*.

          (ii) When reporting a question that has an answer 'Yes' or 'No', use the following structure:

    ask + person addressed + *if* + statement form.

'Statement form' means that we change the question form to the positive sentence form.

(b) a *wh-* question:

    'When is there going to be an election?'

RULE: When there is already a question word (in this example, *when*), use the same formula but instead of using *if* use the question word to connect the two parts:

    He asked him *when* there was going to be an election.

NOTE: The changes of person and verb form are the same as for the statements in Unit 2.39.

(c) imperatives:

    'Prime Minister, call an election.'

RULE: This is a command. Use the verb *ask* to introduce the indirect form. After *ask*, we use the infinitive form:

    He *asked* the Prime Minister to call an election.

We can also use *tell*. This shows a strong command:

    He *told* the Prime Minister to call an election.

NOTE: The passive voice is used when the identity of the person asking the question or giving the command is unimportant:

    The Prime Minister was asked when there was going to be an election.

    The Prime Minister was asked to call an election.

TASK ONE

Andrea Myles is a famous film star. She is holding a press conference in her hotel. Report on the questions the reporters asked her.

For example:
Morning Sun: Where did you go on holiday?
Answer: The reporter from the 'Morning Sun' asked her where she went on holiday.

(a) *Daily Stag*: Are you going to marry Jim Randy?
(b) *Telegram*: When will you make your next film?
(c) *Protector*: Why have you left Apex Films?
(d) *Daily Stun*: How much were you paid for your last picture?
(e) *Daily Wail*: Where are you going for your honeymoon?
(f) *Daily Excess*: Give us a photograph of your new luxury home.
(g) *Tomes*: Must you make a picture with David Rabbit, or can you break that contract?
(h) *Daily Winner*: Stand by the window for a photograph please.
(i) *Tonight*: How are your children now?
(j) *Post*: Have you read the script for your new film yet?

187

TASK TWO

Here is an interview with an Englishman who went to live in Sweden. Report on the questions he was asked.

For example:

The reporter asked him what he liked most about the Swedes.

or

He was asked what he liked most about the Swedes.

Inside out

Nigel Price is a British teacher of English who has been living in Sweden for 11 months.

What do you most like about the Swedes?
They're straightforward, helpful and hospitable.

What do you most dislike about them?
They're difficult to meet and get to know – a bit standoffish.

What do you most respect about the Swedes?
They genuinely want a fair society.

What Swedish characteristics or activities disgust you?
Sometimes they don't help people who need help, especially if they're drunk. They seem to be afraid of getting involved.

What do you think of Swedish women?
They're very, very attractive. They look after themselves, and are more image and health conscious than British women.

What's your impression of Swedish politics?
I haven't been here long enough to get to know the political scene.

Your impression of television?
It's a bit like British television 10 years ago.

What do you think of the sense of humour?
What sense of humour?

What do you think is the favourite hobby of the Swedes?
Deciding where they can't afford to go for entertainment.

In what way is Sweden better than Britain?
There are no poor people. The standard of housing is much better. They're neutral.

How would you rate the following on a scale of 1 (abysmal) to 10 (excellent)? Style: 9. *Promptness of plumbers and repair-men:* 7. *Public transport:* 9. *Road manners:* 4. *Politeness:* 4.

Unit 2.41
INDIRECT SPEECH
Function

The English team said they were over the moon.
She was asked if she had any more of the charity's money.
He asked me to go to Singapore with him.

We use indirect speech when we are:

(a) reporting what someone has said:

(i)   reporting a statement:
      'We are over the moon, now that we've won.
      The English team said they were over the moon . . .

NOTE: *Over the moon* means very happy.

(ii) reporting a question:
      'Have you any more of the charity's money?'
      She was asked if she had any more of the charity's money.

(iii) reporting a request:
      'Go to Singapore with me, Jill.'
      Robert asked me to go to Singapore with him.

**NOTE: Study the use of the pronouns in this example. We change *me* in the request
(. . . with *me* . . .) to *him* in the report (. . . with *him*), because Jill is reporting the
request and the *me* in the request referred to Robert. If Robert reported the question
he asked, it would be different:**
      I asked Jill to go to Singapore with me.

(iv) reporting a command:
      'Stand up!'
      The teacher told the class to stand up.
      The class was told to stand up.

The same rules apply as for the use with requests in the imperative form (see Unit
2.40(c)).

(b) when we are talking about what we are thinking:

Here we can use different verbs to introduce the indirect speech:
  I *think* I saw Rosemary at the cinema last night.
  I *wonder* if I can get to London by midnight.

We can report an interview by saying:
  He asked...
  She replied/answered...

We also use this form after the verb *know*. Here's the first verse of a song:
  I know where I'm going.
  And I know who's going with me.
  I know who I'll love
  But the dear Lord knows who I'll marry.

TASK ONE

Write a report of this interview with Julian Critchley, a Member of Parliament in Britain.

*The*QUESTIONNAIRE

Julian Critchley

JULIAN CRITCHLEY, Conservative MP for Aldershot since 1970, was born on December 8, 1930, the son of a neurologist. He was educated at Shrewsbury School and Pembroke College, Oxford (with Michael Heseltine), and became an MP at the age of 28. A journalist and author, he has just published his first novel, Hung Parliament. Married for the second time, he has three daughters and a son and lives in Farnham, Surrey.

What is your idea of perfect happiness?
Love – after an early supper from Fortnum & Mason.

What is your greatest fear?
Suffocation.

With which historical figure do you most identify?
Rev Sydney Smith – too good a Christian to take religion seriously.

Which living person do you most admire?
Sir Fitzroy Maclean, brave soldier, skilful diplomat, brilliant author.

What is the trait you most deplore in yourself?
Selfishness.

What is the trait you most deplore in others?
Tactlessness (other people telling me I'm selfish).

What vehicles do you own?
Rover 827.

What is your greatest extravagance?
Collecting Staffordshire pottery; daughters' weddings.

What objects do you always carry with you?
Pen, Veganin, comb, Barclays Gold Card.

What makes you most depressed?
Feeling below par.

What do you most dislike about your appearance?
Double chins.

What is your most unappealing habit?
Making jokes at Mrs T's expense.

What is your favourite smell?
Ripe Ogen melons.

What is your favourite word?
Emerald.

What is your favourite building?
The Gatehouse at Stokesay Castle.

What is your favourite journey?
Ludlow to Shrewsbury and back via Bishop's Castle in early summer.

What or who is the greatest love of your life?
South Shropshire.

What do you consider the most over-rated virtue?
Chastity.

On what occasions do you lie?
To save myself, and others, embarrassment.

Which words or phrases do you most over use?
Right.

What is your greatest regret?
That I was never appointed Assistant Postmaster-General.

When and where were you happiest?
1950-1951, Paris. I was a student in love, and had a monthly allowance of £30.

How do you relax?
I sleep after lunch, and read novels.

What single thing would improve the quality of your life?
The remarriage of my first wife!

Which talent would you most like to have?
To be able to play the clarinet (jazz), and write poetry.

What would your motto be?
Roll with the punches.

What keeps you awake at night?
Stomach ache.

How would you like to die?
Swiftly, in a good restaurant, but before the presentation of the bill.

How would you like to be remembered?
By a line on a tombstone in Wistanstow churchyard: "I told you I was ill".

Compiled by Rosanna Greenstreet

TASK TWO

Interview one of your friends and then write a report about the interview.

If it is possible, make a recording of the interview and give it to another friend to write the report.

SECTION 3
Determiners

Unit 3.1
INTRODUCTION

All visitors must report to reception.
They moved to a new house in May.
Ecuador has many beautiful beaches.

Determiners are words which come before nouns and are used to show *which* or *how many* things the nouns refer to, or to show whether a noun refers to a general or specific object, person or place.

There are many determiners but here is a list of some of the common ones:

Articles:	*a, an, the*
Quantity determiners:	*all, some, any, every, one, two, first, second, many, few*
Possessives:	*my, your, her, his*
Demonstratives:	*this, that, these, those*
Wh- determiners:	*which, what, whose*

Examples:

All visitors must report to reception.
They moved to *a* new house in May.
Your English will improve if you practise *every* day.
Ecuador has *many* beautiful beaches.

Many students of English find it very difficult to learn how and when to use determiners, especially articles, but there is one rule you can use:

RULE: Every singular countable noun has a determiner before it in English.

The only exceptions are in some special idiomatic phrases (see the Units in this section and Appendix 3).

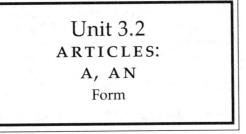

Unit 3.2
ARTICLES:
A, AN
Form

We did an experiment in the chemistry lab.
Raffaele Esposito was a famous pizza maker.

Nouns in English are divided into two main types:

Countable nouns

The first type of nouns refer to things that consist of units. They are *countable* [sometimes called *count* or *unit*] nouns. Examples of *countable* nouns are:

   table, book, house.

These countable nouns always have a singular (for one) form and a plural (for more than one) form.

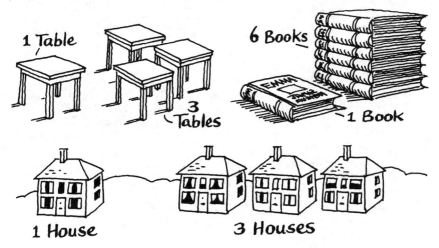

The regular plural is made by adding -*s* to the noun. See Appendix 5 for a list of irregular plurals.

These countable nouns must always have a determiner before them if they are in the singular:

   a table, a book, a house

Uncountable nouns

The second type of nouns refer to something that consist of a mass, or something which cannot be separated out easily, or something which is usually considered as one whole, not its parts. These nouns are called *uncountable* (sometimes *non-count* or *mass* nouns). Nouns which refer to ideas or concepts are also uncountable. Examples of *uncountable* nouns are:

   beauty, steel, water

Uncountable nouns have no plural form and cannot be used with *a* or *an*.

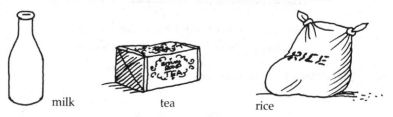

milk   tea   rice

In English there are a few surprising uncountable nouns. The most common are:

money

equipment

furniture

homework

scenery

NOTE: Some nouns which are usually uncountable can be used as countable nouns when they have a special meaning. People use words like 'tea' or 'coffee', which are usually uncountable, in the plural to mean 'cups of tea' or 'coffee', for example when ordering drinks in a coffee shop or café:

   'Two coffees and two teas, please.'

A or an?

We use *a* before consonant sounds:

a book	*a* chair	*a* table	*a* sister
a cat	*a* picture	*a* bed	*a* brother

We use *an* before vowel sounds:

an egg	*an* orange	*an* apple	*an* uncle
an exercise	*an* experiment	*an* example	*an* aunt

Sometimes, a word is spelt with a consonant but it is pronounced with a vowel sound. In that case, we use *an*:

an hour	*an* honest person	*an* X-ray

Sometimes a word is spelt with a vowel but it is pronounced with a consonant sound. In that case, we use *a*:

a unit	*a* European	*a* useful tool

(These three nouns are pronounced with the same initial consonant sound as 'y' in *year*, not with the vowel sound of 'u' in *uncle*.)

TASK ONE

*Put **a** or **an** in front of the following words or phrases:*

accident	hour	experiment
entertaining film	horoscope	hot meal
example	heavy machine	electric current
union	new book	funny cartoon

TASK TWO

*Fill in the correct form of the noun in the blanks in the sentences. If the noun is countable, use the plural form. If the word is uncountable, do not add **-s**.*

(a) The teacher gave them a lot of (homework) .... and no one did it all.

(b) They had to do more (exercise) .... than they usually did and they also had to do (task) .... and (project) ....

(c) The institute has ordered new (equipment) .... for the chemistry laboratory.

(d) The (technician) .... will be able to do more (experiment) .... now.

(e) Many (tourist) .... visit Bali every year to photograph the beautiful .... (scenery), especially the (sunset) ....

(f) I need some (information) .... about (holiday) .... in Switzerland and Greece. Do you have any (brochure) .... ?

Unit 3.3
ARTICLES:
A, AN
Function

Hywel lives in a large house in Leeds.
Janet Kaponicin is an artist.

WHEN TO USE THEM

We use *a* or *an*:

(a) to show that we are referring to a general idea or object and not to a specific example. *A* and *an* are sometimes called 'indefinite articles' because they do not identify a particular noun. They can only be used with singular, countable nouns:
Hywel lives in *a* large house in Leeds.
The house he lives in is not identified or specified.

He went to *a* conference in Singapore last month.
We do not know which particular conference it was.

Pete buys *a* newspaper every day except Sunday.
We do not know which newspaper he buys.

(b) after verbs like *be, seem, become*:
John Corcoran became *a* secondary school teacher in 1961.
Janet Kaponicin is *an* artist.

(c) instead of the number one:
a pound of potatoes (1 pound of potatoes)
a kilo of sugar (1 kilo of sugar)
a hundred kilometres (100 kilometres)
a thousand miles (1000 miles)
In 1975 Austria had only one city with over *a* million people.
The average commuter in London spends *an* hour getting to work (one hour).

(d) to mean *every* or *per*:
John F. Kennedy read 10 or 15 newspapers *a* day (every day).
In the 1970s the average Londoner bought 19 papers *a* week (every week).
A tea plantation worker plucks about 80 pounds of leaves *a* day (per day).

199

TASK ONE

*Put **a** or **an** in the spaces before the nouns in the following passages.*

(a) .... altimeter is .... instrument used in aircraft. It measures the height, or altitude, of .... aircraft above the ground. It measures the air pressure around it to find out the altitude. High above the ground, the air is thin and produces little pressure. So .... low pressure reading means that .... aircraft is flying high. Close to the ground, the air pressure is greater. So .... high pressure reading means that .... aircraft is near the ground.

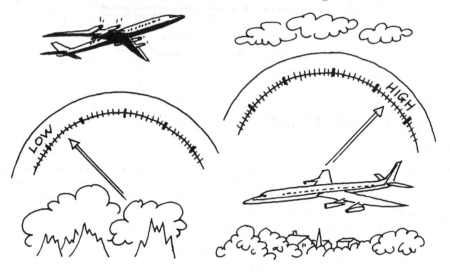

(b) .... plug-in microphone is more convenient than .... microphone which is in .... tape-recorder. Don't put .... microphone on .... unstable table. Use .... appropriate stand, or wrap it in .... clean cloth with the tip out and hold it in .... jar or bottle.

TASK TWO

*Underline the articles **a** or **an** in the following sentences and then put those with the noun which follows it into the box below to show those which are replacing **per** or **every** and those which stand for the number **one**.*

(a) Over half the population of Sweden buys a newspaper a day.

(b) In 1974 British people bought 443 papers a thousand – or a paper for every 2.3 people.

(c) In 1976 Canadians ate less than a kilo of broccoli a year but in 1988 they ate 2 kilos a year.

(d) In 1989 3.9 million Canadians had a computer in their homes. 73 per cent used a computer to play games but 26 per cent also knew how to program. But 33 per cent said they had not used a computer more than once a year.

Per/Every	One

Ashantis name their children according to the day of the week on which they are born.

The first pizzeria was opened in Naples in 1830.

The biggest false-teeth factory in the world is in Liechtenstein.

Potatoes are eaten throughout the world.

WHEN TO USE IT

We use *a* or *an* before a noun to show that it is not a specific or particular one. We use *the* to show that we are referring to a specific or particular noun.

There are three reasons for pointing out that a specific noun is referred to:

(i) The noun has been mentioned before and every time we refer to it again we want to show that it is the same noun:

A new computer tape has been developed by ICI in Britain.

The tape will be used to store data collected from outer space.

The first time the computer tape is mentioned it is *a* tape because it is one of many computer tapes. The second time we use *the* to show that this is the computer tape developed by ICI and not some other tape.

(ii) The noun is made specific because it is followed by a phrase, usually beginning with *of* or *in*, which makes it specific:

The price *of* laptop computers is going down every year.

The men *in* the warehouse are on strike.

Ashantis name their children according to *the* day *of the* week on which they are born.

202

In these examples, *the* shows that 'price' is the specific price of laptop computers, 'men' are the specific workers in the warehouse, and *the* day and *the* week are both specified by phrases after them.

(iii) The noun is specific because it is specified by the context. There are two possible contexts, global and local:

Global contexts are those contexts which are common to all people, such as *the* world and *the* universe.

> *The* earth has a natural satellite – *the* moon.
> *The* sun is a star.
> *The* earth is one of nine planets circling *the* sun.

Our knowledge of the world also tells us that if we use a superlative (see Unit 4.3) we are referring to a specific thing. We use *the* to show this is a specific reference:

> Adrian Moorhouse was *the* first man to swim 100 metres in less than a minute.
> *The* largest lake in Africa is Lake Victoria.
> *The* first pizzeria was opened in Naples in 1830.
> *The* biggest false-teeth factory in the world is in Liechtenstein.

Local contexts are those with which a particular group of people are familiar.
In your own family, you could say:

> It's raining. Please shut *the* window.
> *The* phone is ringing.
> Who's going to feed *the* cat?

The people you were speaking to would know which window, phone or cat you are talking about.

In a school, you could talk about:

> *the* library
> *the* laboratory
> *the* sports field
> *the* Principal

In your own country, you could refer to:

> *the* government
> *the* Minister of Education
> *the* capital
> *the* economy
> *the* weather

All these are references to specific places, people or things which would be known in your country.

Most of the examples in this unit use *the* with singular, countable nouns. We also use *the* with uncountable nouns, or with plural countable nouns if we are referring to a specific noun:

The potatoes I bought come from Idaho.
The milk in that shop is fresh.
The final exams start in May.

If you are making a general statement, do not use *the*:

Potatoes are eaten throughout the world.
Babies need a lot of milk.
Most students worry about exams.

Do not use *the* before these types of nouns:

Names (proper nouns) of people, such as *Peter, Amina, Maria, Charles.*
Names of continents and most countries, such as *Europe, Spain, Asia, Japan.*
Names of cities, lakes and mountains, such as *Rome, Ben Nevis, Everest, Geneva.*
Names of holidays, festivals, days of the week or months, such as *Easter, Monday, January, Christmas, Ramadan.*

We use *the* before these nouns:

Names of countries that start with *United, Republic* or *Federation* or are groups of islands, such as *The United States of America, the Philippines.*
Plural names, such as *The Netherlands, the Smiths* (when more than one member of the family is referred to).
Mountain ranges, such as *the Pyrenees, the Alps, the Himalayas.*
Rivers and canals, such as *the Danube, the Amazon, the Nile, the Mississippi.*
Oceans and seas, such as *the Atlantic, the Mediterranean, the Indian Ocean.*
Deserts, such as *the Sahara, the Gobi, the Nevada.*
Geographical regions, such as *the Middle East, the Caribbean, the Antarctic.*
Newspapers, such as *the Guardian, the Observer, the Times.*

(See Appendices 2 and 3 for further information on this point.)

TASK ONE

*Fill in the blanks in the following passage with **the**, **a** or **an** or with **0** if there should be no article.*

On .... Sunday, 21 April 1991 all .... householders in .... England, ... Scotland and .... Wales had to fill out .... form giving details of everyone who lived at their addresses as .... part of .... 19th full British Census.

.... census is .... national survey to count .... population and collect .... information which .... government departments use to plan .... policies. .... census tries to give .... picture of Britain at .... midnight on April 21. .... people who use .... figures will be able to compare .... results with ....statistics collected in earlier censuses to find out how Britain's population and society are changing.

Most countries count their population. .... United States, for example, has held .... census every ten years since 1790. In 1991, ... census in .... India showed that it has .... total population of 844 million people. Australia's latest census showed that it has 17 million people.

TASK TWO

*Fill in the blanks in the following passage with **the** or with **0** if there should be no article.*

Janet Kaponicin, whose last name means 'Landing Duck' in .... Algonquin language, was raised by her grandmother in .... settlement of .... Baskatong, ... Quebec, ... Canada. Her grandmother taught her .... traditions of .... people which .... artist uses in her art. She uses .... bark from .... birch tree. She separates .... layers of .... bark and then puts them together as collages. Her work is unique in .... North America.

Every person in Britain must fill in the form on Census Day.
No sugar is added to natural orange juice.
The first men landed on the moon in 1969.

All, no, each, every, some, any, much many, several, more, most, little, less, few, fewer, enough, one, two, first, second, last, either, neither.

HOW TO USE THEM

These determiners tells us *how many* or *how much* is referred to:

All is used with uncountable nouns and with countable, plural nouns:
    All electrical equipment should be checked carefully.
    All banks provide a range of services.

No is used with uncountable nouns and with countable plural or singular nouns:
    No sugar is added to natural orange juice.
    No children are allowed to buy cigarettes in Britain.
    No child is allowed to buy cigarettes in Britain.

Each and *every* can only be used with singular, countable nouns:
>Fill in *each* blank in the exercise.
>They interviewed *every* applicant for the job.

Some and *any* can be used with both uncountable and plural countable nouns. A useful 'rule' for beginners is that we use *some* for positive statements and for offers:
>There is *some* tea left.
>There are *some* books on the table.
>Would you like *some* coffee?

and we use *any* for questions and negative statements:
>Are there *any* Malaysian students at Lancaster University?
>There isn't *any* time left to do the task.

Much is only used with uncountable nouns:
>How *much* money do you save every month?
>There isn't *much* time left.

In spoken English, *much* is usually only used in questions or negative sentences. We use *a lot of* in positive statements:
>He has *a lot of* spare time because he has retired from his job.
>Indonesia exports *a lot of* oil.

Many and *several* can only be used with countable, plural nouns:
>*Many* British families take their holidays abroad.
>John Updike has published *several* short poems but he is better known for his novels.

More can be used with countable, plural nouns and with uncountable nouns:
>Austrians buy *more* classical music records or tapes than any other people.
>The World Health Organisation says that we should eat *more* vegetables, fruit and bread or cereals and less sugar, fat and salt.

Most is the superlative form of *more*:
>*Most* milk now consumed by humans is from cows.
>It's the *most* expensive city in the world.

Little is only used with uncountable nouns. It is often used with *very*:
>There is (very) *little* time left.
>He has (very) *little* interest in the subject.

Less is usually used with uncountable nouns. It is the comparative form of *little* and it means a smaller quantity of something:
>There's *less* water in the reservoir this year than last year.
>Americans are eating *less* meat.

Few is used with countable, plural nouns. It is often used with *very*:
>There are (very) *few* American cars in India.
>He has *few* friends.

Fewer is used with countable, plural nouns. It is the comparative form of *few*:
>In 1988 Canadians ate four dozen *fewer* eggs than in 1967.
>*Fewer* people were killed in road accidents in the UK in 1976 than in 1930.

207

NOTE: Many people now use *less* with countable, plural nouns so you will hear people saying:

There were *less* fatal accidents this month than last month.
Less people are buying houses in Britain now.

Enough can be used with countable, plural nouns or with uncountable nouns:
There is *enough* food for everyone.
There aren't *enough* seats for everyone.

WARNING BOX

When *enough* is used as a determiner, it must be followed by a noun and there is no *of* after *enough*:
There is *enough* time to finish the work.
We have *enough* food for everyone.

---

one, two, three, four, etc. (*cardinal numbers*) can only be used with countable nouns. *One* is used with the singular noun and the others are used with plural nouns:
I have only *one* cat.
There are *two* good hotels in Kolhapur
The atmosphere can be divided into *five* layers.

first, second, tenth, etc. (*ordinal numbers*) can only be used with countable, plural nouns:
The *first* men landed on the moon in 1969.
July is the *seventh* month.
She is writing her *fourth* book.

Last can be used to show that something is the final one in a series or the most recent event or time:
I went to Bamako, Mali *last* year.
We bought the *last* bottle of milk in the shop.

Either (. . . *or*) and *neither* (. . . *nor*) can be used with countable, plural nouns or with uncountable nouns:
Malaysian students take *either* arts *or* science subjects in Form 6.
Neither Katie *nor* Jamie has been to Singapore.
She takes *neither* milk *nor* sugar in her coffee and tea.

TASK ONE

(a) *Put* **many** *or* **much** *in front of the following nouns and phrases.*

.... books
.... milk
.... children
.... cars
.... cows
.... coffee
.... cake
.... rice
.... news
.... equipment

.... food
.... chairs
.... people
.... bicycles
.... ice-cream
.... tea
.... sugar
.... carrots
.... information
.... work

(b) *Now list the words and their quantifiers under the two headings:*

There aren't   **There isn't**

For example:

many books   much food

....
....
....
....
....
....
....
....
....

TASK TWO

Put **some** *or* **any** *in the blanks in the sentences below.*

(a) He had .... problems with his work.
(b) Would you like .... orange juice?
(c) I haven't got .... tea but I have .... coffee.
(d) .... Canadians want Quebec to be an independent country.
(e) The authors cover .... topics very well in this chemistry textbook. ....
     chapters are even fun but the authors haven't included .... illustrations.
(f) Did you have .... problems doing this task?

TASK THREE

*Put **all, many, more, most, less, few** or **fewer** in the blanks below. Make sure that the sentences make sense.*

(a) Psychologist Tom Bower says that infants have .... skills than we usually realise. There are .... theories in this area.

(b) .... biologists consider the octopus to be the smartest of .... invertebrate animals, with about the same intelligence as a house cat. .... octopuses belong to a group of molluscs called cephalopods. Octopuses have eight arms; other cephalopods, which include squid and cuttlefish, have ten or .... arms.

(c) .... milk consumed by humans is from cows, although in .... countries milk from buffalo, goats and reindeer is used.

(d) .... doctors believe people in Britain should eat .... fat, sugar and salt and eat .... fresh fruits and vegetables.

(e) There would be .... cars stolen if people had car alarms.

DETERMINERS:
QUANTITY
Function

Most runners in the London Marathon in 1991 finished the race.
There's a little paint left. Let's paint the door.

All, no, each, every, some, any, much, many, several, more, most, (a) little, less, (a) few, fewer, enough, one, two, first, second, last, either, neither, a lot of, lots of.

WHEN TO USE THEM

We use these determiners to show the amount or number of the noun.

Sometimes we give the exact number:
There are *six* rooms in my house.
Pete and Lisette have *five* cats.
There are *74* students in the class.

At other times we may not know the exact number and can use a quantity determiner:
There are *many* students in the class. (written, formal)
There are *lots of* (or *a lot of*) students in the class. (spoken, informal)

We can make the number seem larger or smaller by using different quantifiers. The quantifier you choose depends on whether you think the number is large or small:
There are *six* rooms in my house.
There are *lots of* rooms in my house.
There are *few* rooms in my house.
The number of rooms is six, but you can make this sound like a lot or a few.

Most is another word you can use to influence the reader's or the listener's ideas:
53 per cent of Americans worry about money problems and illness in the family.
This seems to be a precise figure, but would you say:
Many Americans . . . ?
Most Americans . . . ?
Few Americans . . . ?
Some Americans . . . ?

The word you choose makes a big difference. You can make the amount or number seem large or small by choosing different quantity determiners.

WARNING BOX

The meaning of *little* and *few* can be changed by adding *a. Little* means 'a small amount' so it is used with uncountable nouns. If you use *a little,* you mean that there is a positive amount or some:

I have *a little* time so we can finish our discussion.

There's *a little* coffee left in the pot.

If you use *little* without *a* you mean there is not enough. *Very* is often used with *little* to emphasise the negative quantity:

There's (very) *little* time for that.

There's (very) *little* coffee left.

Few means 'a small number' so it is used with countable nouns. If you use *a few,* you mean there are some:

There are *a few* good Chinese restaurants in Lancaster.

She has *a few* friends in Australia.

If you use *few* without *a,* you mean there are not enough. *Very* is often used with *few* to emphasise the negative quantity:

There are (very) *few* good restaurants in Lancaster.

She has (very) *few* friends.

COMMON EXPRESSIONS

NO

No way	to state that some action is impossible.
	There's *no way* I can tell my boss he's wrong. There's *no way* I can finish this in time.
No doubt	to state that you are certain of something.
	There's *no doubt* he's a better athlete.
No problem.	Use this in informal situations to say that something is no trouble to you.
	So you want me to change it? OK. *No problem!*
No need (to do something).	Use this to state that you think someone is acting unreasonably.
	There's *no need to make a fuss* about it.
	Or, use it to state that everything will be all right.
	There's *no need to worry.* Your baby will be all right.
In no time.	Use this to state that something was done very quickly.
	She finished the work *in no time* (at all).
(This is) no time to ...	Use this to state that the subject or action is not appropriate at the moment.
	This is no time to complain when we are all about to lose our jobs.
No time to lose.	Use this to state that something must be done very soon.
	There's *no time to lose* – the decision must be made now.

ANY/NO

Any/no trouble.

Use this to state that you are happy to do something.

A. Thank you for giving me a lift.
B. That's all right. It wasn't *any trouble*/It was *no trouble*.

MANY

Many happy returns (of the day).

Use this to wish someone a happy birthday.

A. It's my birthday today!
B. Well, *many happy returns (of the day)*!

TASK ONE

All, no, each, every, some, any, much, many, several, more, most, (a) little, less, (a) few, fewer, enough, one, two, first, second, last, either, neither, a lot of, lots of.

Choose a suitable quantity determiner from those above, if one is necessary, for each of the blanks in the following texts. Then check with the answers at the back of the book to see if you agree with what the original writers wrote.

(a) .... doctors can combine treating patients with scientific research.
(b) .... aircraft approach an airport at the same time.
(c) By 1851 for the .... time in Britain there were .... people living in towns than in rural areas.
(d) The .... editions of 'the Guardian' newspaper arrive together with those of other newspapers at 11.30 pm. The night news editor checks for .... stories in the other papers that 'the Guardian' does not have. The night duty editor checks 'the Guardian''s edition and may change a .... details.
(e) .... historians need to collect accurate data.
(f) .... young scientist should read 'Advice to a Young Scientist' by Peter Medawar.
(g) .... textbooks are not very entertaining.
(h) .... chapter gives examples and illustrations. The .... part gives tables and charts.
(i) This is the .... book that .... non-specialist astronomer needs to read.
(j) .... books deal with everyday experiences.
(k) .... thought has been given to the impact of 1992 on the developing nations.
(l) .... people agree that Britain's economy has changed over the past ten years, but there is .... agreement over whether the changes have been for the better.

TASK TWO

Look at the following statistics and make statements about the data. Use as many quantity determiners from those above as you can. Then compare your statements with a partner's or with others in the group and see whether you agree.

Trends in Canada
Food consumed (per person per year):
The population of Canada is 25 million.

	1976	1988
broccoli	1 kilo	3 kilos
cauliflower	1.5 kilos	3 kilos
beef	51 kilos	38 kilos
eggs	253	205
breakfast cereal	3 kilos	4.5 kilos
fats and oils	18 kilos	20 kilos
soft drinks	62 litres	90 litres
refined sugar	25 kilos	40 kilos

10 per cent of Canadians took a two-hour sleep during the day.
39 per cent of Canadians spent money on live entertainment.
In 1988 all performing arts companies gave 38 000 performances and 14.5 million people attended.
19 per cent of adult Canadians had a computer in their homes. 47 per cent of all Canadians 15 years and older knew how to use a computer and 82 per cent of those aged 15 to 19 used them. 73 per cent use their computers to play games but 26 per cent also knew how to program. But 33 per cent of Canadians who had computers at home had not used them in the previous 12 months.

For example:
>Canadians ate fewer eggs in 1988 (than in 1976).
>Most (or many or some) Canadian teenagers know how to use computers.

TASK THREE

Think of a subject that interests you and do a survey to find out what other people think or do. You can ask your family, friends, colleagues, classmates, etc. Here is a list of some topics that interest people:

>How people spend their leisure time.
>What people eat.
>What newspapers people read.
>How many books people read every year.
>What music people like best.
>What products people use in their homes.
>What problems people worry about.
>What their opinions are of:
>>television
>>women's rights
>>helpful husbands
>>education
>>travel.

When you have chosen a topic, interview a number of people and make some statements about your survey. If you are studying with a group of people, you could make an oral report on your findings or you could write up the results on a poster. If you are studying alone, then perhaps you could ask an English-speaking person to check your work.

TASK FOUR

Read the following situations and decide which of the common expressions explained in this Unit you would use. Then complete the sentence using that expression.

(a) You have three things to do before lunch. You decide to leave the one that will take a long time to the end and do the other two things first.
>*You:* 'I'll address these envelopes first. I can do that ....'

216

(b) Your friend is going for a job interview but she is very worried about it. You are sure she will get the job.
You: 'There's ……………………… There's ………………………'

(c) You have agreed to spend a weekend with a friend but you find that you have too much work to do and have to finish a report before Monday morning.
You: 'I'm really very sorry but ………………………………'

(d) You are discussing where to go for your holidays with a group of friends. One friend says, 'Look, why don't we forget about going on holiday and just stay home?'
You: 'This ………………………………… We all agreed to go on holiday together.'

(e) You agree to do something for a friend. Your friend says, 'Are you sure it's not too difficult for you to do?'
You: 'Of course not. …………………………………………'

(f) It's your friend's birthday. Everyone is saying 'Happy birthday' but you want to say something different. What can you say?
You: '……………………………………………'

Sign your name on the dotted line.
The bird built its nest in the tree.

My, your, her, his, its, one's, our, their.

HOW TO USE THEM

Possessive determiners refer to pronouns or nouns. They are always followed by a noun:

Pronoun/Noun	Possessive Determiner	Example
I	my	That's my book
You	your	It was your idea.
She	her	This is her pencil.
He	his	Those are his papers.
It	its	The bird built its nest.
We	our	This is our daughter.
They	their	Their son is a lecturer.

(See Unit 5.1 for possessive pronouns which are not followed by a noun.)

WARNING BOX

Its has no apostrophe. *It's* with an apostrophe is short for *it is* or *it has*.

WHEN TO USE THEM

We use *possessive determiners* to show a relationship between someone or something and the noun which follows the possessive:

218

Joan and Michael walk *their* dog every morning.
We know from the use of *their* that the dog belongs to Joan and Michael and that they take it for a walk every morning.

There are 500 000 people in Quebec city and *its* suburbs.
Its here refers to Quebec city.

My refers to the person who is speaking or writing:
 When I was a boy *my* father introduced me to the wonders of opera.

Our refers to the speaker or writer and at least one other person:
 Our family hasn't taken a holiday abroad in six years.
 Our house is on the corner.
Our can also refer to a group of people who have some common purpose or relationship:
 Let's keep *our* children safe on the streets.
 Our beaches are polluted.

Your refers to something related to 'you' and it usually excludes the speaker or writer. It can refer to one person or many people:
 Is this *your* pen?
 You must hand in *your* assignments on Monday morning.
Your also refers to a group of people which could include the speaker or writer:
 Improve *your* environment.

His or *her* refers to a single person:
 She bought *her* car last year.
 He returned *his* books to the library.

Their refers to more than one person:
 They took *their* exams in May.

219

WARNING BOX

Some grammar books tell you that you must use the singular *his* or *her* with determiners like *any*, *every* and *each*:

Each student has *his* own personal tutor.

Every player should do *his* best.

But many people now think that this use of *he* or *his* to include both *he/his* and *she/her* is not acceptable. So most people use a plural *they/their* even with a singular determiner when they are speaking:

Each student has *their* own personal tutor.

Every player should do *their* best.

In writing, you can use *his or her* or *her or his*:

Each student has *his or her* own personal tutor.

Every player should do *her or his* best.

The best way is to put the sentence into the plural:

All students have their own personal tutors.

Players should do their best.

Its refers to animals, things, ideas or places:

The dog wagged *its* tail.

Montreal celebrated *its* 350th birthday in 1992.

One's is a very formal way of saying or writing *his* or *her*. It is not very common in modern English:

The most important thing in business is *one's* reputation for honesty.

Today we would say:

The most important thing in business is *a person's* (or *your*) reputation for honesty.

220

COMMON EXPRESSIONS

Take your pick.	You can choose whatever you like from a selection or group of things.

A: Can I borrow a pencil?
B: Sure. I've got lots. *Take your pick.*

It's your turn to . . . It's my/her/his turn to . . .	Use this when two or more people are doing something one after the other because this is a fair way to share the activity among them. This expression is often used in games and in group work.

It's your turn to do the washing-up tonight.
It's my turn to use the computer.
It's your turn to throw the dice.
It's Peter's turn to report to the class.

Do something my/your/ her/his/their/way.	The person will decide how to do something for her/himself and does not want others to tell her/him what to do or how to do it. There's a famous Frank Sinatra song called 'I Did It My Way'.

A: Let me help you do that properly!
B: Thanks, but I'd rather *do it my way*!

Mind your own business!	A very rude way of telling someone not to interfere or tell you what to do.

A marine biologist, Katherine Muzik, has been studying a coral reef and wants to stop the government from destroying it.

'People tell me to *mind my own business,*' Muzik said, 'but my business is studying living creatures.'

221

TASK ONE

Fill in the blanks in the following passages with **my**, **you**, **her**, **his**, **its**, **one's**, **our** *or* **their**.

(a) Some years ago France Telecom decided to print designs on .... phonecards. The result is a craze for .... cards and some rare ones are now worth up to £3000.

(b) Rudolf Nureyev was born on a Trans-Siberian Railway train near Irkutsk, USSR, on 17 March 1938. .... mother was on a 14-day train trip back from visiting .... husband in the army. .... passport records .... place of birth as Station Razdolnaia. .... family was very poor and some of the stories he told of .... childhood are very sad. Nureyev and Margot Fonteyn hold the record for curtain calls – there were 89 after .... performance of 'Swan Lake' in Vienna in October 1964.

(c) Most moving things stop when they run out of energy: runners stop when .... bodies are tired and a car stops when .... petrol tank is empty.

(d) Good teachers use .... knowledge and experience as tools to help .... students learn well. They are interested in .... students and find ways to guide .... learning. They are not afraid to say there are gaps in .... knowledge but they never stop trying to fill in the gaps.

TASK TWO

Find out some facts about an interesting person you know or about a famous person in your country. Then write a short biography about this person and his or her friends and family.

For example:

My best teacher was a Latin teacher who was more interested in her subject than she was in her students. We always knew that our needs were not very important and that she was not very worried about whether we could pass our exams or not. But her interest in Latin was so great that she made all of us share in her study of Latin and its development. Few students joined her classes but this made our very small group more interesting and very hardworking. One thing about this teacher that increased our fascination was that her eyes were different colours. One was blue and the other was half green and half yellow.

TASK THREE

What could you say in each of the following situations? Use the common expressions that are explained in this Unit.

(a) You have decided to reorganise your filing system. Your friend comes in and says:
   Friend: What a mess! Why don't you do one drawer at a time instead of taking everything out at once?
   You: ....

(b) You are playing 'Scrabble' with a friend. You have put your word on the board but your friend is staring out of the window.
   You: I've put F-R-U-I-T down. ....

(c) You are telling your friend about a private problem you've got when another friend, Bob, joins you, uninvited, and offers advice. You are annoyed by the interruption.
   Bob: Look, if I were you I would do something about it.
   You: ....

DETERMINERS: DEMONSTRATIVES: THIS, THESE, THAT, THOSE
Form and function

This book could change your life.
These smells help people feel refreshed.
That research had great importance.
Those beaches are not safe.

HOW TO USE THEM

Demonstratives come before nouns. *This* and *that* are used before singular nouns or uncountable nouns, and *these* and *those* are used before plural nouns:

Singular	Example	Plural	Example
This	book paper milk rice	These	books newspapers milk bottles rice cakes
That	person child	Those	people children

This and *these* refer to things that are near in time or place.
That and *those* refer to things that are far in time or place.

WHEN TO USE THEM

We use *demonstratives*:
to show which things we are talking or writing about, and also to say whether the things are near or far from the speaker or writer's point of view:

> *This* book could change your life.
> *That* chair in the corner looks broken.

If you go shopping, you refer to the goods that are near you as *this* and *these* and the ones that are farther away as *that* or *those*:

I'll have *this* book and I'd like to look at *those* posters.
I can climb *this* tree but I can't climb *that* one.

To refer to a month or year, we use *this* for the current month and year. If it is March 1992 now, you could say:

I went to Budapest last year (1991) and I'm going to Bucharest *this* year (1992).

or:

I went to Athens last month (February 1992) and I'm going to Oporto *this* month (March 1992).

To refer to the days of the week we use *this* to mean the next time that day comes. If it is Monday, then *this Wednesday* is the day after tomorrow:

I'd like your report by *this* Wednesday.

225

TASK ONE

Fill in the correct demonstrative determiner, **this**, **these**, **that** *or* **those**, *in the following blanks:*

(a) Japanese manufacturers have developed a scented alarm clock. .... clock sprays a smell of pine and eucalyptus into the air 24 seconds before the alarm goes off. Researchers say that .... smells help people to feel more refreshed and alert. So .... people who use .... alarm clock will find it easier to get up in the morning.

(b) About two thousand wild animals are kept as pets in Italy. .... animals often escape from their owners. One family lost a panther near their home outside Rome. The police say .... animal is very dangerous but they have not been able to find it.

(c) Arabian oryx are found in the deserts of Saudi Arabia and Jordan. .... animals were hunted by shooting parties until there were only about 30 left in 1962. Then a zoo in Phoenix, Arizona began breeding .... animals and by 1982 .... zoo and other zoos were able to release .... oryx back into the wild in Jordan.

(d) The paper that .... page is printed on is made out of wood. The wood is mixed with water to make pulp. .... pulp is then rolled out flat and dried. Paper consists of fibres and it is .... fibres which make it so strong.

What colour shirt do you want?

Whose books are on the floor?

Have they decided which city will host the 1998 World Cup?

WHEN TO USE THEM

What, which and *whose* come before singular or plural nouns.

What

What is used when there is no limit put on the number to choose from:

What colour shirt do you want?

What book are you reading?

The speaker did not have any specific number in mind when he or she asked that question.

Which

Which is used when the speaker or writer has a specific number in mind:

Have they decided *which* city will host the 1998 World Cup?

There is a limited number of cities who are bidding for the World Cup.

Which computer did you decide to buy?

Here the speaker knows that the person was making a choice between a known number of different computers.

NOTE: **This 'rule' for *which* and *what* is not always followed. *What* is much more common and people often use *what* even when there is a limited number of choices:**

***What* colour are his eyes?**

***What* computer did you buy?**

Whose

Whose is a possessive determiner:

Whose books are on the floor?

Here the speaker is asking who the books belong to.

Whose car is parked on the grass?

Again the speaker wants to know who the car belongs to.

227

All these determiners can be used as pronouns (see Unit 5.1) if they are not followed by a noun:

He's got a new girlfriend. *What's* her name?
There are some books on the floor. *Whose* are they?
I hear you bought a new computer. *Which* did you get?

TASK ONE

*Put **what** or **which** or **whose** in the blanks in the following sentences.*

(a) .... kind of music do you like?
(b) .... city is bigger, Jakarta or Tokyo?
(c) .... is your name?
(d) I found a pen. .... is it?
(e) .... magazines do you read?
(f) .... mark did you get in the test?
(g) He doesn't know .... car to buy.
(h) .... colour is your cat?
(i) .... dictionary do you use?
(j) I've got a red and a blue pen. .... do you want to borrow?

TASK TWO

Answer these questions about yourself and then ask one or two other people the same questions. Fill in the chart and see in how many ways you are like the others.

Question	You	Friend 1	Friend 2
What colour are your shoes What is your favourite colour? Which newspaper do you read? What soft drinks do you like? Which TV programmes do you watch? Whose music do you like?			

Add some more questions of your own.

229

SECTION 4
Modification

Unit 4.1
ADJECTIVES
Form

It's a large dining-room.
That's a small kitchen.
Don't leave broken bottles around.
That dress is expensive.
Books are not cheap nowadays.

HOW TO USE THEM

Large, small, broken, expensive and *cheap* in the above examples are adjectives.

Position

(a) They can come before the word they describe:
   It's a *modern* kitchen.
   Don't leave *broken* bottles around.

(b) They can come after certain verbs, such as *be, seem, become,* etc., when they describe the subject (see Unit 1.1):
   That dress is *expensive.*
   Books are not *cheap* nowadays.
   She became *angry* with him
   Suddenly he seemed very *old.*

NOTE: When we are talking about something specific, and we are using the verb *be*, we can express the idea in both ways:
   That dress is *expensive.*
   It was an *expensive* dress.
This about one particular dress. When we are talking generally, then we can only use the form in (b):
   Books are not *cheap.*
This is a comment about all books.

Form

Adjectives do not change – they are the same for the singular and plural:
   The *old* farmer lived in the village.
   The *old* farmers met in the market square on Thursdays.

232

Connecting more than one adjective

Sometimes we use more than one adjective to describe something or someone:

> Shirley Temple was a *rich, famous* child.
> A *tall, young Italian* woman stood in the doorway.

When they come before the noun, it is often only necessary to put a comma between them. When they come after a verb and describe the subject, then we usually put *and* before the last adjective:

> Shirley Temple was *rich and famous*.
> The woman in the doorway was *tall, young and Italian*.

Types of adjectives

There are five main types of adjectives.

(a) **Subjective** adjectives
These tell us what the speaker or writer thinks. Other people may disagree:

> You get a *beautiful* view from the top of the hill.
> You don't, if it's cloudy!
> That's a very *expensive* book.
> Not for a book with so many famous pictures.

(b) **Characteristic** adjectives
These adjectives describe things which exist:

> *age*   (the *old* man)
> *size*   (the *small* town)
> *shape*   (the *round* tower)
> *colour*   (the *blue* sky)

(c) **Proper name adjectives**
Some adjectives are formed from proper names:

> *Indian* restaurant
> *Australian* farms

(d) **Materials** adjectives
These adjectives tell us what things are made from:

> a *plastic* bag
> *cotton* socks

(e) **Purpose** adjectives
These adjectives tell us the purpose of the noun:

> a *swimming* costume
> a *hunting* dog

Order of adjectives

There is no absolute rule about the order for adjectives, but this chart will give you some idea:

	Subjective	Characteristic	Proper names	Materials	Purpose	Noun
a	lovely	old	Chinese			vase
		large		wooden		box
	cheap				army	coat

NOTE: Adjectives in the *characteristics* column have no fixed order. The order of subjective and characteristic adjectives is often changed:

a *beautiful, large, red* chair.
a *large, red, beautiful* chair.

The order is decided by the feature the speaker thinks is most important. This will come first.

TASK ONE

Rewrite the following sentences so that the adjectives come after the verb and describe the subject.

For example:
    Frank has a large, brown car.
    Frank's car is large and brown.

(a) Jess has a small, green car.
(b) She was a clever, young girl.
(c) It was a long, boring book.
(d) It's a cold, wet part of the country.
(e) Juliet has three lively and imaginative children.

TASK TWO

Insert the following adjectives into the text.

**bright   modern   young   tall   handsome   shy   pretty   strong   warm
sunny   blue   old   retired   charming**

When I got on board the .... ship, I looked at my fellow travellers and tried to guess who they were. There was a .... couple, a ...., ... man with a ...., ... girl. They were on their honeymoon. Then I saw a .... man walking towards me. He was the ship's sportsman. Every .... morning before breakfast, he ran round the .... deck in his .... shorts. Further along the deck there was the .... couple from the cabin next to mine. I guessed the .... man was a .... vicar with his .... wife. These were my companions for the next few weeks. When I met them that night, I was wrong about all of them.

235

Unit 4.2
ADJECTIVES
Function

The sea is blue.
Charles is rich and clever.
Vanessa is always interesting.

WHEN TO USE THEM

We use adjectives:

(a) to describe things or people:
   The sea is *blue*.
   The sky is *overcast*.
   Charles is *rich and clever*.
   Vanessa is always *interesting*.

(b) to identify things or people:
   I want the *small, red* book
   They live in the house with the *green* door.

COMMON EXPRESSIONS

To be browned off	to feel depressed.
To be yellow	to be a coward.
To feel blue	to be sad.
To be green with envy	to be jealous.
To be green	to be naive.
To be black and blue	to be bruised or hurt.

236

TASK ONE

Make up sentences to describe the people or objects in column one using the adjectives in column two. You should use more than one adjective. See how many sentences you can make and compare yours with other people in your group.

For example:

    It's an old, wooden house.
    The house is old and wooden.

If you are using a person's name, then the name must come at the beginning of the sentence.

For example:

    Darren is young and tall.

chair house Darren garden Mabel	old, leather, young, poor, large, pretty, tall, small, funny, expensive, cheap, beautiful, colourful, wooden, untidy, ugly, boring, dull, calm, clean, healthy, strong, weak

TASK TWO

With a partner, choose five things in the room. Without naming the objects, write down something about each one.

For example:

    something round and blue.

Then give your list to another pair. They will try to identify what you have chosen.

They can ask you questions if they cannot guess.

For example:

    Is it near the window?
    Can you touch it?

TASK THREE

Which colour is used to describe someone who:

(a) feels sad
(b) doesn't know very much
(c) is very envious
(d) is badly bruised
(e) is a coward.

Unit 4.3
ADJECTIVES:
COMPARISON
Form

The cheaper plates are over there.
We put the bigger boys in the rugby team.
The oil made it dirtier.

HOW TO FORM IT

When we use adjectives in sentences in its standard form, such as *cheap*, *big*, *dirty*, we call this the *positive* form of the adjective. When we want to compare things or people, we can use another form of the adjective, called its *comparative* form, or we can add *more*.

Comparative form

(a) Short adjectives
With *short* adjectives, we make the comparative form by adding *-er* to the stem:
  The *cheaper* plates are over there.
  We put the *bigger* boys in the rugby team.
  It was never a pleasant beach, but the oil made it *dirtier*.

NOTES: With adjectives that end in *-y*, such as *happy* and *dirty*, we change the *y* to *i* and add *-er*, as in *happier*, *dirtier*.
With some short adjectives, such as *big*, *red*, *fat*, we double the last letter and add *-er*, as in *bigger*, *redder*, *fatter*.

Positive	Comparative
happy	happier
ugly	uglier
red	redder
hot	hotter

238

(b) Long adjectives

With *long* adjectives, we put *more* before the adjective:

> It's *more expensive* to travel on Fridays.
> It's *more dangerous* on the southern slope.

NOTE: When we are comparing two things, we can also use *(not) as . . . as*:

(i) things which are the same:
> **It's very cold this year. It's *as cold as* it was in 1985.**

(ii) things which are not the same:
> **Gas is *not as dear as* electricity.**

Or, we can use . . . -*er than*:
> **Electricity is cheap*er than* gas.**
> **Electricity is *not* cheap*er than* gas.**

Superlative form

(a) short adjectives

For the superlative form, we add -*est* to the stem:

> Rutland was the *smallest* county in Britain.
> The Rhine is one of the *dirtiest* rivers.
> Tessie O'Shea was the *fattest* woman in films.

The rule for adjectives ending in -*y* and some short adjectives like *big*, etc. is the same as for the comparative form.

(b) Long adjectives

With long adjectives we put *most* before the adjective:

> Who is the *most beautiful* girl in the world?
> Rory Underwood is England's *most successful* rugby player.

WARNING BOX

The superlative form is always preceded by *the* or a word that shows we are not speaking generally, such as *England's* in the last example (see Unit 3.4).

Irregular adjectives

Some short adjectives have irregular comparative and superlative forms. Here are the common ones:

Positive	Comparative	Superlative
good	better	best
bad	worse	worst
little	less	least
many	more	most
old	older/elder	oldest/eldest

TASK ONE

From the information given in Unit 4.3 complete the following chart.

Positive	Comparative	Superlative
hot		
		coldest
	more dangerous	
		worst
lucky		
	larger	
comfortable		
		most pleasant
	happier	
little		
	younger	
		thickest
thin		
		loveliest
important		

241

He built a house as big as a mansion.
My grandma is older than grandad.
Everest is the highest mountain in the world.

WHEN TO USE IT

Comparative form

We use the comparative form to compare:

(a) people or things:
He built a house as big as a mansion
His house is *bigger*.
The *older* cars were *better*.

(b) people or things that are the same:
He built a house *as big as* a mansion

(c) people or things that are not the same:
My grandad is *not as old as* my grandma.
My grandma is *older than* grandad.
Van Gogh's paintings are *more expensive than* Picasso's.
Picasso's paintings are *not as expensive as* Van Gogh's.

Superlative form

We use the superlative form when we compare one person or thing with others in a group, or when we are talking about a special characteristic that is unique:
Everest is *the highest* mountain in the world.
The Queen of England is one of *the richest* people in the world.
Britain's *most violent* man left prison ten years ago.

COMMON EXPRESSIONS

The more the merrier.	It's better to have a lot of people. It doesn't matter if you bring some friends to a party.
The sooner the better.	You should do something as soon as possible.
As old as the hills.	Use this to describe something that is very old.
As good as gold.	Use this to describe someone who is very well-behaved, especially a child.
All the best.	Use this to wish someone well when you say goodbye to them.

TASK ONE

Here is a consumer report on garden ornaments. Read through the report and then complete the table below. The following information has to be inserted into the table:

4 kgs   5 kgs   1 metre   £10   £15   £17   £30   very poor   very good

We looked at garden ornaments. In our 'best buy' category, the cheapest were Gardenguard, but for weather-resistance they were among the poorest. The heaviest were Rosepixie, and they were also the most expensive. The tallest were Gnomeland, but they were lighter than Rosepixie and cheaper than Majorette, which were among the best for weather-resistance.

Product	Weight	Height	Price	Weather-resistant
Gardenguard	2 kgs	20 cms		
Gnomeland				good
Littlemen	1.5 kgs	15 cms	£12	poor
Majorette	3 kgs	25 cms		
Rosepixie		15 cms		good
Wonderland	2.5 kgs	10 cms	£20	very good

244

TASK TWO

Here is a report on a consumer survey for 'Outside wall protection cover' for your house.

We found six makes for our 'best buy' category. The .... of these was Enclose, the .... was Fight. It cost £12.86. Wallsafe was also expensive, but it was the .... and one of the .... Fight was the .... effective. Keepoff cost .... than Wallsafe per litre and was just as effective.

This report has left out these adjectives.

cheap   expensive   large   effective   little   small   much   good

By referring to the following table, insert the adjectives in their proper form (comparative or superlative) and in the appropriate places.

Product	Price	Size	Effectiveness
Dirtway	£10.56	3 litres	good
Enclose	£3.73	2 litres	poor
Fight	£12.86	3 litres	excellent
Keepoff	£8.0	4 litres	very good
Safewall	£6.60	2.5 litres	very good
Wallsafe	£12.00	5 litres	very good

TASK THREE

Go to your local shop or market. Make a survey of the different makes of one product on sale there. Write a report similar to the ones in TASKS ONE and TWO.

TASK FOUR

How would you respond in these situations? Use the common expression that are explained in this Unit.

(a) A friend asks how well-behaved their child has been while you have been looking after the child.
(b) A colleague at work asks you when you want the report he is preparing.
(c) A friend asks you if she can bring some friends to your party.

246

It was an interesting book.
He was an interested spectator.

HOW TO USE THEM

Adjectives ending in -*ing*

Adjectives ending in -*ing* describe the person, animal or thing and tell us how another person feels about them:

'The Role of Majesty' was an *interesting* book for Diana.
Keith thought Liza was *boring*.
Pit-bull terriers are *frightening* dogs.
Dick was a *fascinating* man.

Adjectives ending in -*ed*

Adjectives ending in -*ed* can only be used for people or animals. They show how a person or animal feels towards someone or something else:

Marilyn is an *interested* spectator at the quarrel between the head and the staff.

This shows how Marilyn felt about the quarrel. We could say this in another way:

The quarrel was *interesting* for Marilyn.

Here is a picture of a *frightened* child.
The child is *frightened* by the cat.
The cat is *frightening* to the child.

Very often adjectives ending in -*ed* are followed by a preposition:

The child was *frightened by* the cat.
He was *interested in* seeing the film.

247

The following table shows the prepositions that usually follow adjectives ending in -ed:

	At	By	In	Of	With
amazed	√	√			
amused	√	√			
annoyed	√				√
astonished	√				
bored		√			√
confused		√			
depressed		√			
disappointed	√	√			√
disgusted	√	√			√
embarrassed		√			
excited		√			
fascinated		√			√
frightened	√	√		√	
horrified	√	√			
interested		√	√		
involved			√		√
satisfied		√			√
shocked	√	√			
surprised	√	√			
terrified	√	√		√	
tired				√	
worried		√			

TASK ONE

Complete the following sentences by using one of the adjectives listed.

**amusing   tired   frightening   interesting   surprising   worried   amazed
interested   amazing   bored**

(a) Burgess writes .... books.
(b) Alice was .... at the way Bix played jazz.
(c) The athlete was very .... after running the marathon.
(d) A very .... Juliet left the dull party early.
(e) The end of the film was ....
(f) For a small child, a large playful dog might be ....
(g) The .... mother went to the police about her lost child.
(h) The speaker was met by a group of very .... people who wanted to hear
     what he had to say.
(i) Cher arrived at the party wearing an .... dress.
(j) Larsen draws very .... cartoons.

TASK TWO

With a friend, think of a film, book or famous sightseeing place.

(i) *One person writes down all the adjectives they can, describing what you have chosen.*
(ii) *The other person writes down all the adjectives which describe how they feel about the film/book/
place. This person must also add the appropriate preposition after the adjective.*

For example:
     I liked it very much. It was interesting and surprising.
     I didn't like it. I was bored by it. I was surprised by the bad architecture.

She came late.
They danced beautifully together.
Julian spoke in a lively way.

HOW TO FORM THEM

Single word adverbs

There are two types of single word adverbs.

(i) Some, such as *soon, already, often,* are not related to any other words (see Unit 1.6).

(ii) Others are related to adjectives. In most cases, it is possible to form an adverb from an adjective by adding *-ly* to the adjective:
> Their dancing was *beautiful.* (adjective)
> They danced *beautifully* together. (adverb)
Similarly, we have:

Adjective	Adverb
beautiful	beautifully
quick	quickly
stupid	stupidly

NOTES: When the adjective ends in *-y,* such as *funny,* change the *-y* to *-i* and add *-ly*:
> *funny funnily*
> *happy happily*
Some adjectives, such as *late* and *hard* do not change.
> He caught the *late* train. (adjective)
> He arrived *late.* (adverb)
> He's a *hard* worker. (adjective)
> He works *hard.* (adverb)

250

WARNING BOX

The adverbs *lately* and *hardly* do exist, but they are not derived from *hard* and *late* and have different meanings:

  lately means *recently*.
  hardly means *only just*.

There are some irregular adverbs which are formed from irregular adjectives, such as the adverb *well* from the adjective *good*:

  This book is *good*. (adjective)
  The students behaved *well*. (adverb)

Multi-word adverbs

We often call groups of words used as an adverb *adverbials*. Many are formed with prepositions. There are two types:

(i) When an adjective ends in -*ly*, we make the adverbial with a prepositional phrase:

  Walter was a very *lively* man. (adjective)
  He did everything *in a lively way*. (adverbial)

Adjective	Adverbial
lively	in a lively way
ugly	in an ugly way
silly	in a silly way

(ii) Some adverbials are prepositional phrases and are not connected to adjectives. (See Unit 4.8 for examples.)

251

HOW TO MAKE THE COMPARATIVE FORMS

We call the standard form of an adverb, such as *beautifully, funnily, happily*, the *positive* form of the adverb. Only adverbials formed from adjectives have a *comparative* and *superlative* form. They are usually formed in the same way as long adjectives (see Unit 4.3). For comparatives, we put *more* before the adverb and for superlatives we put *most*:

Positive	Comparative	Superlative
beautifully	more beautifully	most beautifully
quickly	more quickly	most quickly
in a lively way	in a more lively way	in a most lively way

WARNING BOX

Well, the adverb from *good*, makes its comparative and superlative form like *good*:
    GOOD – BETTER – BEST (adjective)
    WELL – BETTER – BEST (adverb)

Well is also an adjective meaning 'not ill':
A. How are you?
B. Very well, thank you.

TASK ONE

Rewrite the following sentences changing the adjectives to adverbs.

For example:

She's a beautiful painter.	She paints beautifully.
His behaviour is very friendly.	He behaves in a friendly way.

(a) The tennis star was a fierce competitor.
(b) That baby has a lovely smile.
(c) Professor Mo is a bad lecturer.
(d) He's a good footballer.
(e) That book tells a good story.
(f) Her behaviour was very strange.
(g) He has a loud voice when he speaks.
(h) They made a beautiful film.
(i) She's a hard worker.
(j) It's a friendly cat.

TASK TWO

Think of five people you know and describe how they do things.

He's already here.
He works quickly.
He drives fast.
She spoke in a lively way.
They'll come at ten o'clock.
The horse jumped over the fence.

WHEN TO USE THEM

Adverbs tell us something more about the action. They modify the verb and answer questions about the action.

How?

Most adverbs that come from adjectives answer the question *how?*
A. How does he work?
B. He works *quickly*.

A. What's she like when she gives a lecture?
B. Oh! She speaks *in a* very *lively way*.

When?

There are a few single-word adverbs that answer the question *when?*
A. When will they arrive?
B. They'll be here *soon*.

Often, the question *when?* is answered by a prepositional phrase:
A. When will they arrive?
B. They'll be here *at ten o'clock*.

Where?

You must always use a prepositional phrase as adverbial in answer to the question *where?*
A. Where has Frankie gone?
B. Frankie's gone *to Hollywood*.

How often?

These questions are usually answered by single-word adverbs (see Unit 1.6):
  They *never* come here.
  They *often* visit Portugal.

COMMON EXPRESSIONS

The sooner the better.   Use it when you would like something done as soon as possible.

Better late than never.   It is better to do something late than not do it at all.

TASK ONE

Complete the following sentences by adding an adverb or adverbial which answers the question at the end of the sentence.

For example:
A. They will arrive. *(When?)*
B. They will arrive *at ten o'clock.*
   They will arrive *soon.*

(a) They came. *(When?)*
(b) Joanne spoke. *(How?)*
(c) Martyn was standing. *(Where?)*
(d) The horse ran in the race. *(How?)*
(e) The young man went to see the old lady. *(How often?)*
(f) The sailor helped the old lady into the lifeboat. *(How?)*
(g) The nurse took the child. *(Where?)*
(h) I'll see you. *(When?)*
(i) I've met him. *(How often?)*
(j) Come up and see me. *(When?)*

TASK TWO

Think of some people you know and describe how they do things.

┌─────────────────────────────┐

Unit 4.8
PREPOSITIONAL
PHRASES
Form and function

I'll see you in April.
The boy stood on the corner of the street.
She stood by the window.

HOW TO USE THEM

For time

(i) With months and seasons, we use *in*:
    I'll see you *in* April.
    I went to Malaysia *in* the summer.

(ii) For days and dates, we use *on*:
    You must hand in the project *on* 22 February.
    I shall be away *on* Friday.

(iii) For times on the clock and short festivals, we use *at*:
    I came here *at* one o'clock.
    My mother and aunt stayed with me *at* Christmas.

WARNING BOX

Note the following expressions:
    in the morning
    in the afternoon
    in the evening
but
    at night.

In Islam, Ramadan lasts for a month, so we say '*in* Ramadan'. This is because it is a long period, not a short one like Christmas and Easter in the Christian religion.

257

(iv) To show the last possible time that something can be done or something will happen, we use *by*:

    You must finish this *by* Friday.
    He'll be here *by* five o'clock.

For place

Position

IN

    She was standing *in* the shop.

NOTE: We also use *in* for weather:
    She went for a walk *in* the rain.
    The children played *in* the snow.
    The English like lying *in* the sun.

ON

    They could see him *on* the roof.

NOTE: Be careful about this difference:
    The chair is *in* the corner of the room.
    The boy stood *on* the corner of the street.

BY/NEAR

    The killer stood *by* the window.
    The killer stood *near* the window.

258

WARNING BOX

When talking about travelling, we say:

    by car
    by train
    by bicycle
    by plane
    by ship
but
    on foot.

Other prepositions of place showing position are *under* and *above*:
    The boy hid *under* the table.
    The file is on the shelf *above* the piano.

Movement

INTO

    She was going *into* the shop.

ON TO

    They could see him climbing *on to* the roof.

OUT OF

    He got *out of* the car.
    She came *out of* the house.

Other prepositions showing movement are *over*, *to* and *towards*:
    The horse jumped *over* the fence.
    They're going *to* New York for their holidays.
    The thief is running *towards* the river.

TASK ONE

Complete the following story by putting the appropriate prepositions into the gaps.

It was .... the evening .... Friday 29th March .... Tribeca, New York. Police patrolman Swaine and assistant patrolman Bradley were driving .... 3rd Avenue. Swaine stopped the patrol car, which was new and shining, ... an electrical store. He needed some batteries. He got .... and went .... the store; but he left the keys .... the car because Bradley stayed .... the car. Swaine looked .... the street. It was crowded .... early evening shoppers. It was brightly lit and lively.

Suddenly, the door .... the driver's seat opened and a young man got .... the car. 'I gotta go,' he said. Bradley wasn't sure what was happening. As the young man tried to start the car, Bradley held .... the gear stick. Soon the two men were struggling .... the front .... the car.

Every evening Dave Merry went .... a ride .... his bike. He did it mainly .... exercise, but he also enjoyed going .... the city .... bike. He liked weaving .... and .... the traffic. .... this evening, he saw the two men struggling .... the front .... the car. He got .... his bike and ran .... the car.

Meanwhile, a man .... the corner .... the shop saw what was happening and told patrolman Swaine. Swaine ran .... the shop. He saw the cyclist banging .... the car. He thought he was the criminal. He pulled him .... the car. The cyclist fell .... the ground. He was astonished and started struggling with Swaine. Then Swaine saw the fight .... the car. He freed himself .... the cyclist. He got .... and went .... the car. He pulled open the door. Soon the criminal was overcome.

The Queen of England is a very rich woman.
It was too hot to sit in the sun.
The man was old enough to be her father.
There was enough food to feed an army.

HOW TO USE THEM

TOO, VERY

Too and *very* are used with adjectives and adverbs only. They come before the adverb or adjective they are qualifying:

> The Queen of England is a *very* rich woman.
> The party went on *very* late.
> It was *too* hot to sit in the sun.
> The train arrived *too* late for him to go to the meeting.

NOTE: With *too*, there is usually a qualifying comment afterwards.

ENOUGH

Enough can also be used with nouns.

(i) *Enough* comes after an adjective or an adverb:
> The man was old *enough* to be her father.
> The film will finish early *enough* for us to have a meal afterwards.

(ii) *Enough* comes before the noun it is qualifying:
> There was *enough* food to feed an army.
> Is there *enough* time to have a coffee?

261

TASK ONE

*Complete the sentences with **too**, **very** or **enough**.*

(a) He was .... late to go to the party.
(b) She was old .... to go to see the film alone.
(c) It was a .... exciting book.
(d) There weren't .... chairs for everyone at the meeting.
(e) It's .... hot at Christmas in Australia.
(f) The old lady didn't like summer in North Africa. It was .... hot for her.
(g) London is a .... big city.
(h) I don't like her ideas but I think she's a .... clever politician.
(i) When their leader died, the people became .... violent.
(j) Is it warm .... for you? I can put the heating on if you're cold.

The invitation arrived too late for him to go to the party.

John worked very hard.

He had enough money to last his whole life.

He was old enough to see the film on his own.

HOW TO USE THEM

ENOUGH

We use *enough* to show the right amount:

Marcus was old *enough* to see the film on his own.

In Britain there are some films you cannot see if you are under fourteen, unless you go with your parents. Marcus is now over fourteen, so he can see the film.

Paul McCartney has *enough* money to last all his life.

Paul McCartney does not need to earn any more money.

263

VERY

We use *very* to emphasise the situation or condition. It shows that there is more than enough:

> The Queen is a *very* rich woman.

By this we mean that even for rich people, the Queen is richer than most.

> John worked *very* hard.

John worked harder than most people.

TOO

We use *too* to show that something is in excess and something else has happened because of this:

> The invitation came *too* late for him to go to the party
>   (event)   (result)

We can say this in a different way:

> The invitation came so late that he couldn't go to the party.
> She was *too* important to travel tourist class.
>   (situation)   (result)

We can say this in a different way:

> She was so important that she didn't travel tourist class.

COMMON EXPRESSIONS

It's never too late.	There is always time to do something, even a new career, whatever your age.
All too true!	It is absolutely true, unfortunately.
Too bad!	Use this when something has gone wrong for a friend. You are sorry but not very interested.
Very much so!	This shows strong agreement.
Enough is enough!	Use this to show something should stop or is finished.
That's enough!	Often said angrily to show that something should stop.
Enough said!	The speaker has made her/his point and there is no need to say any more.

TASK ONE

*Find captions for these pictures, using **too**, **very** or **enough**.*

For example:

He's too short to reach the shelf.
She's tall enough to reach the shelf.

TASK TWO

*Put **too**, **very** or **enough** in the spaces.*

Tim Merlyn is a .... strange man. The people where he lives think he's ....
mean. He's .... mean to give money to help the poor, although he is .... rich.
He has a house which is big .... for two families to live in but he never offers help
to the homeless. He never goes out and is always .... angry when someone knocks
on his door.

TASK THREE

*Write a short paragraph like the one in TASK TWO about someone. It can be someone you know or
an imaginary person.*

TASK FOUR

*Write down your response to the following situations. Use the common expressions that are
explained in this Unit.*

(a)   Someone is telling you about a friend who has done something wrong. Finally you
      don't want to hear any more. You tell them to stop.
      You:

(b)   A friend tells you that someone you know has lost her job. The friend doesn't think
      this is possible. But you know the story is true. You tell her it is.
      You:

Unit 4.11
RELATIVE CLAUSES: SUBJECT: WHO, WHICH, THAT
Form

The man who came to dinner.
The cat that caught all the mice in my house.
The jewellery which belonged to my mother.

HOW TO FORM THEM

Here are two sentences:
> The man stayed forever.
> He came to dinner.

They are both talking about the same person who is the subject of both sentences. *He* in the second sentence is *the man* in the first one. *We* can join these two sentences together:

> The man *who came to dinner* stayed forever.

Here we have changed *he* in the second sentence to the pronoun *who* and put that sentence after *man*, which it describes.

Who, which or that

When we are talking about people, we use the pronoun *who*:
> She's the person *who won the prize*.

For animals and things, we use the pronoun *which*:

> We have sold the jewellery *which belonged to my mother*.

We can use *that* for people, animals and things:
> The cat *that caught all the mice in my house* . . .
> The man *that came to dinner* . . .
> The jewellery *that belonged to my mother* . . .

NOTE: Although we often use *that* when referring to *people*, some people consider this to be impolite.

TASK ONE

Match the people and things on the left with the descriptions on the right.

(a)	the man	who loved dancing
(b)	the woman	which lost the race
(c)	the jewels	which was flooded by the sea
(d)	the horse	who scored three goals in the football match
(e)	the fox	which sang sweetly
(f)	the girl	who played golf before tea
(g)	the boy	which was haunted
(h)	the house	who always drank a lot of tea
(i)	the town	that ate the chickens
(j)	the bird	which belonged to the Queen

TASK TWO

Insert each of the following clauses into an appropriate place in the story underneath. Decide whether to put **who** *or* **which** *in front of the clause. The first one has been done for you.*

is a small village in Kyushu
is one of the islands of Japan
was the owner
was very tall
were of people and places in the USA
walked with him
belonged to one of his friends
was in the main street running through the village
administered the village
were friends of his
was just along the road
seemed to be telling me his life story
was inside
were woken by the noise

Many years ago I went for a holiday in Aoshima, **which is a small village in Kyushu**. In the evening I went to a small restaurant, ... It was a cold evening and the restaurant was empty. After a while, a man, ... came in. He saw me and started to talk. Later a few other men .... came in. They joined him and started to talk to me. I couldn't speak any Japanese and only the owner could speak English but that didn't stop them – especially one man .... and .... With everything he said, he pointed to himself. After a while, the owner brought out his projector and started to show us photographs .... He hadn't been to the USA but he liked collecting photographs from there. When this was finished, the group took me to the fire station, ... The very tall man was the local fireman. The man .... was the local policeman. I realised I was with the people .... The fireman opened the doors to the fire station and proudly showed us the beautiful fire engine .... He wanted to give me a ride on it. He gave me a helmet .... Everybody got on the fire engine and we were soon racing round the village sounding the alarm. Many people .... came out of their houses to see where the fire was. We all thought it was very funny.

```
┌─────────────────────────────────┐
│  ┌───────────────────────────┐  │
│  │       Unit 4.12           │  │
│  │  RELATIVE CLAUSES:        │  │
│  │      OBJECT               │  │
│  │       Form                │  │
│  └───────────────────────────┘  │
└─────────────────────────────────┘
```

I cannot give up the woman I love.
That's the car I sold last week.

Sometimes the common factor between the two sentences is the object and not the subject:

  I cannot give up the woman.
  I love her.

The man is talking about the same woman in both sentences. We can join them together in several ways:

When we are talking about people, the form considered to correct for the relative pronoun is *whom*. But *whom* is formal and we do not often use this form.

  I cannot give up the woman *whom* I love. (formal)

When we speak or write, we usually use *who*:

  I cannot give up the woman *who* I love. (usual or informal)

or we use nothing at all, called a 'zero relative' or '∅ relative':

  I cannot give up the woman *I love.* (usual)

For animals and things we use *which*. This is always the same for formal and informal:

  That's the car.
  I sold it last week.

The car is the object in the second sentence. We can join them together like this:

  That's the car *which* I sold last week. (usual)

or

  That's the car *I sold* last week. (usual)

NOTE: In both cases we can also use *that*:
  I cannot give up the woman *that* I love.
  That's the car *that* I sold last week.

270

TASK ONE

Answer the questions or comments below by making the answers suggested into a relative clause.

For example:

Who was that woman?
   I met her at the opera.

Answer:

That's the woman (who) I met at the opera.
or

She's the woman (whom) I met at the opera.

(a) What's that book?
   I bought it last week.
(b) Who's that man?
   I saw him at your office.
(c) What a nice car!
   They bought it last year.
(d) What's this picture of a hotel?
   I stayed at that hotel on holiday.
(e) I'm sorry, but I've broken that ornament.
   I bought it in Japan twenty years ago.
(f) It's a very strange house.
   Jack built that house.
(g) What a dull game!
   I like the game very much.
(h) Who was King Harold?
   William of Normandy defeated him in 1066.
(i) I liked the film 'Citizen Kane'.
   I saw it twenty years ago.
(j) Those are interesting drawings.
   A Polish student gave them to me.

┌─────────────────────────────────┐
│   │
│   Unit 4.13   │
│   RELATIVE CLAUSES: │
│   GENITIVE: │
│   WHOSE, OF WHICH   │
│   Form   │
│   │
└─────────────────────────────────┘

'The Guardian' whose readership rose last year . . .
The club of which 70 per cent of the members were over 60 . . .
The boy whose father went to gaol . . .
The book, the name of which I can't remember, . . .

HOW TO USE THEM

Read these statements and follow the arrows.

The boy is sad.

His father is in gaol.

When the link between two sentences is a possessive determiner (see Unit 3.7), we use *whose* or *of which* to join them to form one sentence. If it is a person, then we use *whose*:

The boy *whose* father is in gaol is sad.

We can also use *whose* with things:

'The Guardian' . . .

Its readership rose last year.

This becomes

'The Guardian' *whose* readership rose last year . . .
('The Guardian' is a newspaper published in Britain.)

However, we often use *of which* with things:

That club is the oldest in the town.
Seventy per cent of the membership is over 60.

To join these, we use *of which*:

That club, *of which* 70 per cent of the membership is over 60, is the oldest in the town.

272

Sometimes we put *of which* after the noun the possessive determiner was qualifying:
>The book gives a good account of the spice trade.
>I can't remember its name.

This can be joined as:
>The book, the name *of which* I can't remember, . . .

Similarly we could say:
>The club, seventy per cent of the membership *of which* is over 60, . . .

WARNING BOX

We never use *that* as a possessive relative.

273

TASK ONE

Answer the questions or comments below by making the answers suggested into a relative clause.

For example:

Who's that woman?

Her husband owns the grocer shop on the corner.

Answer:

She's the woman whose husband owns the grocer shop on the corner.

What a lovely house!

Its owners want to pull it down.

Answer:

That's the house the owners of which want to pull it down.

(a) What a strong man!

His father worked in a circus.

(b) What did you think of the book?

Its plot was trivial.

(c) I know that girl. Who is she?

Her mother is the headteacher.

(d) Is that woman a pilot?

Yes, her father taught her to fly.

(e) What do you know about this painter?

His brother gave him a lot of money.

(f) Who's that man over there?

His poems are very popular.

(g) Do you know the speaker?

Her talks are very lively.

(h) What do you know about the composer of this music?

His music is rarely played nowadays.

Unit 4.14
RELATIVE CLAUSES
Function

the men who ruled India . . .
Gandhi, who Churchill imprisoned, . . .
the car that was in an accident . . .
In the house that Jack built . . .
The boy, whose father was sent to prison last year, . . .

WHEN TO USE THEM

(a) We use a relative clause to describe people or things and to identify them:
 A. Which men are you talking about?
 B. I'm talking about the men *who ruled India during the time of the British Empire.*
Here the second speaker is identifying the people he is talking about.

 A. Where will you live?
 B. In the house *that Jack built.*
Once again the second speaker is identifying something by explaining where she will live.

 A. Do you know that boy?
 B. Yes, he's the boy *whose father was sent to prison last year.*
Here the second speaker is identifying the boy.

(b) When the people or objects are known and it is not necessary to identify or describe them, we can use a relative clause to give additional information. This is always the case when we are talking about a named person or named place:
 Gandhi, *who Churchill imprisoned*, was assassinated in 1948.
In this case the clause *who Churchill imprisoned* is additional information.

Gandhi is well known as the person who led India to independence from Britain in 1947, so it is not necessary to identify or describe him.

When we use a relative clause for this purpose we must put commas (, . . . ,) at each end of it.
 India, *which has over 600 million people,* is called the biggest democracy on earth.
The clause *which has over 600 million people* is not necessary information to identify India.

275

That man, *whose name is Roth*, owes me £1000.

The clause *whose name is Roth* is not important as the speaker has identified the man by pointing him out using 'That man . . .'.

WARNING BOX

When we use the relative clause to give additional information, we cannot use the 0 relative for the object. We must use *who, whom, which* or *that*.

TASK ONE

Decide the function of the relative clause in each of the following sentences and make changes in the punctuation where necessary.

For example:
   The director *who made 'Psycho'* was an Englishman.

Here there is no need to make any changes as the relative clause **who made 'Psycho'** *is necessary to identify the director.*
   Alfred Hitchcock, *who made 'Psycho'*, was an Englishman.
Here we must put commas around the clause **who made 'Psycho'** *because it does not identify Alfred Hitchcock, but gives us more information about him.*

(a)   Switzerland which has four national languages is in the centre of Europe.
(b)   The man who I met last night was very boring.
(c)   Don whose wife has been ill for two years has decided to take her for a long holiday.
(d)   That picture which you painted in Japan is very beautiful.
(e)   I don't like the people who live at the end of the street.

TASK TWO

Insert these clauses into the paragraph below. You must decide whether to put **who, whom, which, that, whose** *or nothing in front of the clause. The first one has been done for you.*

was again very warm and sunny	the children poured over themselves
the hotel owner recommended	mothers were carrying large bundles of clothes
was both a bathroom and a laundry	they had brought with them
was in the hills	

We decided to spend the weekend, **which was part of a long independence holiday**, in a small hotel .... where it would be cooler. We arrived late on Friday evening and went straight to bed. On the Saturday morning, ..., we went to a nearby pool, ... It was surrounded by rocks and seemed to be very private. Soon after we arrived, a lot of children came. They were followed by their mothers. The children, ..., quickly undressed and jumped into the pool. Then their mothers threw them some large bottles. The bottles contained some soapy water .... Then the mothers undid the bundles of clothes .... and started to wash them and scrub them on the rocks nearby. From being a place for a quiet swim, the pool became a place, ... The children were very happy, and laughed and shouted as they washed each other. The mothers sang quietly as they washed their clothes. We sat quietly at the edge of the pool. We didn't know what to do.

TASK THREE

Write a short paragraph like the one above about a place you know well or have visited.

SECTION 5
Connecting

He ran the London Marathon.
I only played against her once.
These books are ours.

HOW TO FORM THEM

PERSONAL PRONOUNS

Personal pronouns have a different form for subject, object and possessive forms. The chart below sets out the different forms:

Subject	Object	Possessive
I	me	mine
you	you	yours
he	him	his
she	her	hers
it	it	its
we	us	ours
they	them	theirs

NOTE: The possessive pronouns *my, your, his, her, its, our, their* which come before a noun are possessive determiners (see Unit 3.7).

WARNING BOX

Note that the pronoun *its* has no apostrophe. *It's* means *it is* or *it has*.

Examples:
I gave *him* the book.
He ran the London Marathon.
It's a pleasure to *him*.

280

I only played against *her* once.
These books are *ours*.
Is this pen *yours* or *mine*?

REFLEXIVE PRONOUNS

Reflexive pronouns refer back to the subject. The singular form *-self* is used with singular object pronouns *my, your, him, her, it*:

I wanted to do it *myself* but he insisted on helping me.
She fell off the ladder and injured *herself*.
At the Peto Institute in Budapest my son learnt to dress *himself*.
You can do these tasks by *yourself* or with a partner.
After five minutes it will automatically turn *itself* off.

WARNING BOX

We don't usually add a reflective pronoun when we talk about *dressing, washing* or *bathing* grown-up people or adults. But we do use *himself/herself* for young children, especially when they first learn to do these things.

The plural form *-selves* is used with the object pronouns *our, your, them*:

Let's buy *ourselves* a chair for the garden.
We want you to enjoy *yourselves* while you are here.
They built the house *themselves*.

WARNING BOX

Note that it is *themselves* and not * *theirselves*.

INDEFINITE PRONOUNS

Some, any and *every* can be combined with *-one, -body* or *-thing* to form *indefinite pronouns*:
anyone, anybody, anything
someone, somebody, something
everyone, everybody, everything.

No can be combined with *-body* or used with *one*:
nobody, no-one

In both British and American English, every*one*, any*one* and some*one* are used more often than every**body**, any**body** and some**body**.

The indefinite pronouns *anyone, anybody, everyone, everybody, someone, somebody, no-one* and *nobody* are grammatically singular but many people, even in formal English, follow these pronouns with a plural pronoun:

Everyone must return *their* books to the library before the end of the week.

If you use the singular, then you have to say:

Everyone must return *his or her* books to the library before the end of the week.

The best way to avoid the problem is to put the subject in the plural:

All members of the library must return *their* books before the end of the week. (See Unit 3.7 for more on this topic.)

DEMONSTRATIVE PRONOUNS

The demonstrative pronouns *this, these, that, those* can have words like *all, both* and *half* before them:

All these are for sale.
We need *both those*.

But the construction with *of* is much more frequently used:

All of these are for sale.
We need *both of those*.

WARNING BOX

When *all, both* and *half* are followed by *of* and a noun, you must use the article *the* or the demonstratives *this* or *that, these* or *those*:

all of these books
both of those boys
half of the pages

When the quantity determiners, *some, any, many, few*, etc. are used with *of* and a noun, you must also use the article *the* or the demonstratives *these* or *those*:

some of the people
many of those students
most of these books

DETERMINERS AND PRONOUNS

Many words, such as:

all	some	each	both	some	any	enough
much	many	this	that	these	those	little
less	least	one	more	most	either	neither
which	what	whose	no	few	fewer	several

can be either *determiners* (see Units 3.5 to 3.9) or *pronouns*. We can tell the difference between two forms by checking whether the word is followed by a noun or not. Determiners are always followed by a noun; pronouns stand alone as they refer to the whole noun phrase in these cases:

Determiner	Pronoun
Many people in Britain are vegetarian.	But *many* continue to eat meat.
Which sports do you watch on television?	*Which* do you go to watch in person?

In the first example, *many* used as a pronoun stands for 'many people'; in the second example, *which* used as a pronoun stands for 'which sports'.

TASK ONE

Fill in the blanks in the following chart.

Subject	Object	Possessive	Reflexive
I	me	....	myself
you	you	....	....
....	him	....	himself
....	her	hers	....
it	it	....	....
we	....	ours	ourselves
you	....	....	....
they	....	theirs	....

TASK TWO

Complete these sentences using pronouns.

(a) I did it ....
(b) She gave .... to ....
(c) We made the dinner ....
(d) They bought .... in Singapore.
(e) She tried to finish ....
(f) My pen is blue; .... is green. This pen is blue so it is ....
(g) Don't give your cats a bath. They wash ....
(h) They enjoyed .... at the party.
(i) He saved his money so he could buy .... a bicycle.
(j) I can't do this. Can .... help me?
(k) These instructions are very clear. .... can do this experiment.
(l) .... knows some words in English like *okay, hi* and *bye*.
(m) .... of the students passed the exam.
(n) Can you tell .... the time?
(o) It rained so .... went for a walk.

TASK THREE

Put the correct form of the pronoun in the blanks in the passages below.

(a) Inside a flower, bees collect nectar with their tongues. Then .... take .... back to the hive.

(b) When their daughter first saw the sea, ... said, 'What is ....?'

(c) If you are working for ...., ... should start a pension now. The sooner .... start the more .... benefit.

284

(d) A man in Jakarta sold pencils to students. .... told .... that the pencils would give the correct answers automatically. But many students failed .... exams and .... complained to the police. .... paid £220 for each pencil.

(e) Anne Billson says, 'There are four things .... hate about pop music. .... is too loud. .... all sounds the same. The lyrics are stupid. And the people who sing .... look like idiots. My parents hated .... too. The difference between .... and .... is that .... were never pop fans but .... was once.'

Unit 5.2
PRONOUNS
Function

They have five children.
This is a city of 3.6 million people.
I want to stay in this job for life.

WHEN TO USE THEM

Pronouns are used:

(a) in place of a noun:
   Billy Graham and Ruth were married in 1943. *They* have five children.

Here *they* replaces Billy Graham and Ruth to avoid repetition of their names.

   In 1977 Katherine Whitmire was elected mayor of the city of Houston, Texas in the United States. *This* is a city of 3.6 million people.

Here *this* replaces Houston to avoid repeating the name.

(b) to replace a noun phrase:
   Most people can't hold their breath for more than a minute. But pearl divers in Japan train themselves to do *this* for up to five minutes underwater.

Here *this* replaces 'hold their breath'.

   If he thinks he's romantic, let him prove *it*.

Here *it* replaces 'that he is romantic'.

(c) to refer directly to the outside world or situation:
   We all know that smoking is harmful.
   You need to plan now for your future.

Here *we* and *you* are not replacing nouns in the text. They refer directly to people outside the text itself.

286

TASK ONE

In the following passages there are no pronouns. Replace the nouns and the noun phrases with pronouns wherever you think it is possible.

(a) Andrew moved out of Andrew's house last month because Andrew was getting very tired of the noise from the dogs in the house next to Andrew. The dogs barked all day and night. The dogs barked when the dogs heard a noise and the dogs barked when the dogs didn't hear a noise. The dogs were very big dogs and the dogs made a lot of noise when the dogs barked. Andrew tried using ear plugs at night to keep out the noise but the ear plugs made Andrew's ears ache. Now Andrew is living in a flat in a building where dogs are not allowed.

(b) Steve Crone bought Steve Crone's first llama eight years ago from a convent. The llama was a problem because the llama attacked the nuns. 'The llama was a problem child,' Steve Crone explained. 'The llama was raised by humans so the llama thinks Steve Crone is a llama too.' Now the llama is the leader of Crone's herd of eight llamas. The llamas live in the state of Maine in the United States. Steve Crone and Steve Crone's wife and Steve Crone and Steve Crone's wife's children live in Maine because Steve Crone and Steve Crone's wife run a business taking people on hikes through the mountains on the llamas.

(c) Angela Rippon says that Angela Rippon uses a personal stereo. Angela Rippon doesn't wear the personal stereo in the street. Angela Rippon is learning French so Angela Rippon uses the personal stereo to improve Angela Rippon's French. Angela Rippon says Angela Rippon listens to a tape for ten minutes every day. In the gym when Angela Rippon exercises on the walking machine, Angela Rippon plays pop music. Angela Rippon walks in time to the music beat. Walking in time to the beat helps Angela Rippon to keep going.

TASK TWO

Find any piece of writing that has a lot of pronouns in it. Put the nouns back in the passage and then get your partner to replace the nouns with pronouns. You can do the same with your partner's passage. This will help you practise using the correct pronouns. When you finish, check with the original passage. The best place to find a passage with a lot of pronouns is in articles about people or biographies and autobiographies.

Unit 5.3
SO, NEITHER/NOR
Form and function

> 'Is David coming?'
> 'I think so.'
> 'I've just seen Kevin.'
> 'So have I.'

HOW TO USE THEM

So and *neither–nor* are used like pronouns (see Units 5.1 and 5.2), but instead of replacing a noun, they replace a phrase:

    A. 'Is David coming?'
    B. 'Yes, I think *that David is coming.*'

It is not usually necessary to repeat the information in the question, and we replace 'that David is coming' with *so*:

    B. Yes, I think *so.*

Let's continue the dialogue:

    A. 'How do you know he's coming?'
    B. 'He said *so.*' (He said that he was coming.)

In addition to the verbs *think* and *say,* there are other verbs that can be followed by *so*:
    He *hopes* so.
    He *does* so.

In the *negative*, we replace *so* with *not*:

    A. 'Is David coming?'
    B. 'I hope *not.*' (I hope he isn't coming.)

Similarly we can say:
    He does not.
    She says not.

288

WARNING BOX

When we use *think* in the negative, we do not use *think* + *not*. We use *don't* + *think*:

A. 'Is David coming?'
B. 'I *don't think* so.'

Another occasion when we use *so* is when we want to show agreement or show that a situation is the same:

    A. 'I like cheese.'
    B. '*So* do I.'

    A. 'He's going to Paris next week.'
    B. '*So* is she.'

    A. 'I've finished the work.'
    B. '*So* have I.'

Here, we begin the sentence with *so*, which is then followed by the part of the question form (see Unit 1.2). We do not use the main verb after *so*:

    so + auxiliary + subject

When the main verb in the sentence is in the negative, we use *neither* or *nor*:

    A. 'He hasn't finished the work.'
    B. '*Neither* has she.'

or

    '*Nor* has she.'

Both forms are correct.

TASK ONE

Complete these short dialogues.

For example:
    'Will it rain this afternoon?'
        'I think ....' (negative)
Answer: 'I don't think so.'

(a) 'Has Mary brought the food with her?'
       'I hope ....' (positive)
(b) 'How do you know Marc has got the job?'
       'He said ....' (positive)
(c) 'Is the rent for the flat expensive?'
       'I think ....' (negative)
(d) 'Is Lizzie ill?'
       'I think ....' (positive)
(e) 'Is Tom in the team?'
       'I hope ....' (negative)
(f) 'Will the train be on time?'
       'They said ....' (positive)
(g) 'Is Margaret going to Morocco this year?'
       'She said ....' (negative)
(h) 'Is it true that Graham has a lot of money?'
       'No, he does ....' (negative)
(i) 'Have they booked the tickets for the opera?'
       'I hope ....' (negative)
(j) 'Did Dickens write "The Woman in White"?'
       'I think ....' (negative)

TASK TWO

Here is some information about four countries. Write sentences to show how they are similar to each other.

Poland	Britain	Hungary	Japan
mid-continent	island	mid-continent	island
Europe	Europe	Europe	Asia
poor	rich	poor	rich
37 860 000 people	57 080 000 people	10 600 000 people	122 610 000 people
312 683 sq. km.	244 100 sq. km.	93 036 sq. km.	377 800 sq. km.

290

For example:
> Poland has less than 40 million people. So has Hungary.
> Japan is bigger than 300 thousand square kilometres. So is Poland.

TASK THREE

Get some information about your friends or people who live near you and describe their similarities, such as their ages, heights, sports, jobs. How many brothers and sisters do they have? Where did they spend their holidays last year? Then write sentences like those you wrote in TASK TWO.

> **The twins were only fourteen years old and lived alone.**
> **The twins were only fourteen years old, but lived alone.**
> **He stopped the car and went into the showroom.**
> **He went into the showroom, but forgot to lock the car.**

And and *but* are used to join two sentences together. Each original sentence has the same value.

AND

When we use *and* for events, the order of the events in the sentence shows the order in which they happened:

> He stopped the car.   He went into the showroom.
> He stopped the car *and* went into the showroom.

If the subject of the two sentences is the same, we don't repeat it when we join the two sentences together.

And also joins two sentences which state facts about someone or something:

> The twins were only fourteen years old. They lived alone.
> The twins were only fourteen years old *and* lived alone.

BUT

By using *but*, we show that we are surprised by the information or that it is something unexpected:

> The twins were only fourteen years old.   They lived alone.
> The twins were only fourteen years old, *but* lived alone.

We are surprised that such young people are living alone.

> He went into the showroom.   He forgot to lock the car.
> He went into the showroom, *but* forgot to lock the car.

We use *but* because we expect people to lock their cars when they leave them.

But shows a contrast from normal expectations.

292

TASK ONE

*Connect the sentences in the following groups using **and** or **but**.*

For example:

It was a lovely day.   She went for a walk in the hills.
It was a lovely day **and** she went for a walk in the hills.

He paid a lot of money for the holiday.   The hotel was very poor.
He paid a lot of money for the holiday **but** the hotel was very poor.

(a) The children enjoyed the school.
      They went there early every day.
(b) The writer wasn't very good.
      She made a lot of money from her books.
(c) Everest was a great challenge to climbers.
      Many people tried to climb it.
(d) Andy liked children.
      He and his wife didn't have any.
(e) The author of 'Danton's Death' died at 23.
      He is very famous.
(f) It rains a lot in the northwest.
      It's a good place for a holiday.
(g) He looked ugly in the painting.
      He liked it.
(h) The mountain was very high and dangerous.
      She climbed it.
(i) Rome is a lovely city.
      It attracts many visitors.
(j) I have very little money.
      Could I buy the picture over there?

She didn't come because it rained.
She didn't come because of the rain.

When we want to say why things happened, we can do it in different ways.

BECAUSE OF

Because of is a preposition and is followed by a noun or pronoun:
    She didn't come *because of* the rain. (*because of* + noun)
    Botham hurt his leg and couldn't play *because of* it. (*because of* + pronoun)

NOTE: We can also use *due to* and *owing to* in this way:
    ***Due to* the injury to his leg, Botham couldn't play.**

BECAUSE

Because is a conjunction and is followed by a clause:
    She didn't come *because* it rained. (*because* + clause)
    Because he hurt his leg, Botham couldn't play. (*because* + clause)

NOTES: We can also use *since* and *as* to show the reason why something has happened:
    ***As* he hurt his leg, Botham couldn't play.**
    Botham couldn't play *since* he hurt his leg.

The part of the sentence governed by *because of* or *because* and their alternatives *due to/owing to* and *since/as* can come at the beginning or the end of the sentence.

TASK ONE

*In each pair of sentences below, one of the sentences gives the reason why the other happened. Join them together with **because of** or **because**. If it is possible, use both forms.*

For example:
> The weather was very hot.
> > Barry ate a lot of ice-cream.

> Because the weather was very hot, Barry ate a lot of ice-cream.
> Because of the hot weather, Barry ate a lot of ice-cream.

(a) It was raining heavily.
> The gardener didn't come.
(b) The book was very long.
> He couldn't finish it.
(c) The child was very heavy.
> The mother couldn't lift her.
(d) The farmer didn't know the man.
> The farmer thought he was a thief.
(e) There were many complaints about her work.
> She lost her job.

TASK TWO

Write down the reasons for each event in the picture story.

Start at the end of the story and work backwards.

For example:
> The boys became ill because they ate the fish.

295

I'll see her after she's spoken to the director.
She'll come to see you before she leaves.
I'll be working in the library while you're playing tennis.
I was working on the book when the news came.

WARNING BOX

Although the speaker might be referring to the future, the part of the sentence that follows a time conjunction, such as *after, before, when, while*, uses the present simple or the present perfect.

There are many conjunctions which link sentences together and show the *time* relationship. The common ones are *after, before, when* and *while*.

AFTER

I'll see her *after* she's spoken to the director.

In this statement, one event follows another:

First, she will speak to the director.
Second, I will see her.

She will speak to the director.	*I'll see her.*
1	2

We have used *after* to join these sentences, so it is the second event which is the more important.

BEFORE

She'll come to see you *before* she leaves.

Again there are two events, where one follows the other:

First, she'll see you.
Second, she'll leave.

She'll see you.	*She'll leave.*
1	2

This time we have used *before* to join these sentences, so it is the first event which is the more important.

WHILE

I'll be working in the library *while* you're playing tennis.

I'll be working in the library.

You'll be playing tennis.

Here there are two events, but this time the use of *while* shows they are happening at the same time. The part beginning with *while* is not so important for the speaker.

WHEN

I was working on the book *when* the news came.

	The
I was working on the book.	*news*
	came.

In this example, the part of the sentence beginning with *when* interrupted the main part of the sentence.

TASK ONE

Complete the sentences below by putting in one of the time conjunctions **after, before, when, while.**

(a) He was watching television .... the accident happened.
(b) The cat left the mouse at the door .... she had killed it.
(c) They left the car by the canal .... they went to look for the boat.
(d) .... he was going to London to see his girlfriend, she was going to Cambridge to see him.
(e) .... you buy a new radio, you should find out which is the best.
(f) He was climbing a mountain .... he hurt his leg.
(g) The woman phoned her husband .... she got the news.
(h) They were working in the garden .... the storm broke.
(i) .... he left the house, he checked that everything was safe.
(j) You were sailing on the canal .... I was painting the house.

TASK TWO

Look at how you have completed the sentences in TASK ONE and decide in each case how the events occur. Put (a), (b), etc. in the appropriate place in the box.

THE MAIN EVENT IS FIRST	
THE MAIN EVENT IS SECOND	
THE TWO EVENTS ARE HAPPENING TOGETHER	
THE MAIN EVENT IS INTERRUPTED	

TASK THREE

When you are reading or listening to English, note when these conjunctions are used and how they are used.

298

Appendix 1
IRREGULAR VERBS

There are more than 150 verbs in English that do not form the *past* and the *past participle* by adding *-ed* to the stem or infinitive form. They are called *irregular verbs*. But many of these verbs aren't very common. This chart only contains the words that are in common use. There is a group of verbs that have two forms for the *past* and *past participle*. Generally, in British English, the *irregular* form is used but in American English the *regular* form is more usual.

Present simple/infinitive	Past simple	Past participle
Verbs with both regular and irregular forms		
	British/U.S.	**British/U.S.**
burn	burnt/burned	burnt/burned
dream	dreamt/dreamed	dreamt/dreamed
lean	leant/leaned	leant/leaned
learn	learnt/learned	learnt/learned
smell	smelt/smelled	smelt/smelled
spell	spelt/spelled	spelt/spelled
spill	spilt/spilled	spilt/spilled
spoil	spoilt/spoiled	spoilt/spoiled
Verbs with irregular forms		
be	was/were	been
beat	beat	beaten
become	became	become
begin	began	begun
bend	bent	bent
bet	bet	bet
bite	bit	bitten
blow	blew	blown
break	broke	broken
breed	bred	bred
bring	brought	brought
broadcast	broadcast	broadcast
build	built	built
burst	burst	burst

Present simple/infinitive	Past simple	Past participle
Verbs with irregular forms *(continued)*		
buy	bought	bought
catch	caught	caught
choose	chose	chosen
come	came	come
cost	cost	cost
cut	cut	cut
deal	dealt	dealt
dig	dug	dug
do	did	done
draw	drew	drawn
drink	drank	drunk
drive	drove	driven
eat	ate	eaten
fall	fell	fallen
feed	fed	fed
feel	felt	felt
fight	fought	fought
find	found	found
fly	flew	flown
forbid	forbade	forbidden
forget	forgot	forgotten
forgive	forgave	forgiven
freeze	froze	frozen
get	got	got *(British)*
get	got	gotten *(American)*
give	gave	given
go	went	gone/been
grind	ground	ground
grow	grew	grown
hang	hung	hung *(for objects)*
hang	hanged	hanged *(for people)*
have	had	had
hear	heard	heard
hide	hid	hidden
hit	hit	hit
hold	held	held
hurt	hurt	hurt
keep	kept	kept
know	knew	known
lay	laid	laid
lead	led	led
leave	left	left

Present simple/infinitive	Past simple	Past participle
Verbs with irregular forms *(continued)*		
lend	lent	lent
let	let	let
lie	lay	lain
light	lit/lighted	lit/lighted
lose	lost	lost
make	made	made
mean	meant	meant
meet	met	met
pay	paid	paid
put	put	put
read	read	read
ride	rode	ridden
ring	rang	rung
rise	rose	risen
run	ran	run
say	said	said
see	saw	seen
seek	sought	sought
sell	sold	sold
send	sent	sent
set	set	set
sew	sewed	sewn/sewed
shake	shook	shaken
shine	shone	shone
shoot	shot	shot
show	showed	shown
shrink	shrank	shrunk
shut	shut	shut
sing	sang	sung
sink	sank	sunk
sit	sat	sat
sleep	slept	slept
slide	slid	slid
speak	spoke	spoken
speed	sped/speeded	sped/speeded
spend	spent	spent
split	split	split
spread	spread	spread
spring	sprang	sprung
stand	stood	stood
steal	stole	stolen
stick	stuck	stuck

Present simple/infinitive	Past simple	Past participle
Verbs with irregular forms *(continued)*		
sting	stung	stung
strike	struck	struck
swear	swore	sworn
sweep	swept	swept
swim	swam	swum
swing	swung	swung
take	took	taken
teach	taught	taught
tear	tore	torn
tell	told	told
think	thought	thought
throw	threw	thrown
understand	understood	understood
wake	woke	woken
wear	worn	worn
weave	wove	woven
win	won	won
wind	wound	wound
write	wrote	written

Compound verbs ending in *irregular* verbs form the *past* and the *past participle* in the same way as the irregular verb:

Present simple/infinitive	Past simple	Past participle
overcome	overcame	overcome
undertake	undertook	undertaken
upset	upset	upset

The is used with nouns or noun phrases to refer to a whole group of people:

(a) *The* is used with nouns of nationality that refer to a whole group of people of one nationality or ethnic group:

> *the* Americans, *the* Algerians, *the* Arabs, *the* Australians, *the* Belgians, *the* Brazilians, *the* Canadians, *the* Chinese, *the* Danes/Danish, *the* Ethiopians, *the* French, *the* Finns/ Finnish, *the* Germans, *the* Indians, *the* Peruvians, *the* Saudi Arabians, *the* Swedes/ Swedish, *the* Swiss, *the* Venezuelans.

When the nationality nouns end in *-sh* or *-ch* you must use *the*:

> *the* Spanish
> *the* French.

Nationality nouns with *-sh* and *-ch* endings can also be used as adjectives:

> Danish pastry
> French bread

When nationality nouns end in *-s, the* is optional so you can omit it if you prefer:

> (*The*) Tanzanians speak at least two languages.

When *-s* nouns are used as adjectives, they drop the final *-s*:

> *Brazilian* music is popular with both (*the*) *Brazilians* and with foreigners.

(b) We can also refer to a whole group of people by using *the* and an adjective:

> *the* rich/poor
> *the* unemployed
> *the* handicapped

(c) Some names are always preceded by *the*:

(i) Plural names in general:

> *the* Philippines
> *the* United States
> *the* Smiths
> *The* Netherlands

(ii) Geographical names:

Mountain ranges (plural and singular):
    the Alps
    the Andes
    the Himalayas
    the Caucasus
(Mountain peaks are not preceded by *the*):
    Everest, Annapurna, Pike's Peak

Groups of islands:
    the Canaries
    the Bahamas

Rivers:
    the Volga
    the Amazon

Oceans and seas:
    the Atlantic (Ocean)
    the Red Sea

Canals:
    the Panama Canal
    the Suez Canal

Other geographical features followed by an *of* phrase:
    the Isle of Wight
    the Straits of Gibraltar

(iii) Public institutions and facilities:

Government:
    the Ministry of Education
    the Senate
    the Royal Exchange

Universities (only when they include an *of* phrase):
    the University *of* Lancaster
    (but Lancaster University)

    the University *of* Malaya
    (but Oxford University,
    McGill University,
    Harvard University)

THE TAJ GROUP OF HOTELS

The Westmorland Gazette

THE UNIVERSITY OF BIRMINGHAM

The RSPB

LANCASTER UNIVERSITY

304

Museums, libraries, etc.:
    the British Museum
    the National Library
    the BBC

Hotels:
    The Ritz
    The Merlin Hotel

Theatres, cinemas, clubs, etc.:
    the Odeon
    the Yacht Club

(iv) All newspapers and some journals:
    The Independent
    The Guardian
    The Economist

The is part of the name of these newspapers and periodicals and is usually spelt with a capital letter. If, however, another determiner is used before the name, then *the* is omitted:

    Have you seen *my* Economist?
    Where is *today's* Guardian?
    I'd like *a* Times and *a* Telegraph please.

Most magazines and many journals, however, have no *the*:
    Time, Nature, TESOL Quarterly, Newsweek, Good Housekeeping, Reader's Digest.

In the following charts, the left column lists common expressions that do not have any article or, as it is sometimes said, use *zero article*. The right column lists examples of the same words in other contexts when they do have an article.

Institutions of life and society

With zero article (idiomatic use)	With an article (normal use)
be in / go to / get out of { bed, class, hospital *(British English, not American)*, prison, jail, town }	Don't sit on the bed. The class start at 2.00. The hospital is near the prison/jail. The town is very old.
be at / go to { school, sea } be in/be at church	We visited the school. He sat by the sea and dreamed. They are building a new church in the town.
go to { college, university }	The college was opened last year. The university is outside the city.
live on/off campus	It has quite a large campus.

306

Means of transport and communication

With zero article (idiomatic use)			With an article (normal use)
travel leave come go	by	bicycle bus car boat ship train plane	She bought a bicycle. Take the blue bus. You could win a car. We built a boat. The ship sails at noon. The train left at 1.00. The plane is delayed.
communicate/ communication	by	radio telephone telex/fax post *(British)* mail *(American)* satellite	Turn on the radio. May I use the telephone? He sent a telex. The post has arrived. Has the mail come? You can't see the satellite.

Times of day and night

With zero article (idiomatic use)		With an article (normal use)
at	dawn/daybreak sunrise/sunup sunset/sundown noon/midnight dusk/twilight	Let's watch the dawn. The sunrise was lovely. He's watching the sunset. I'm going in the afternoon. It's hard to see in the twilight.
at/by before after all	night morning/noon/evening dark/nightfall/midnight day/night/week/year	I woke up in the night. In the evening we watched a film. Cats can't see in the dark. It will take him a week to do the work.

Seasons

The article is usually omitted when we speak of seasons generally but not when we refer to a particular year.

With zero article (idiomatic use)		With an article (normal use)
in	(the) spring/summer/winter/autumn (*fall* in American has *the*)	The summer of 1985 was very cold.

Meals

The article is usually omitted when we refer to meals as a routine or social institution but not when we refer to one particular meal:

We always have dinner at 7.30.

But,

I had *a* huge dinner yesterday.

With zero article (idiomatic use)		With an article (normal use)
come for have before after at/for	breakfast lunch/dinner tea supper brunch/drinks/cocktails	They serve a good breakfast. The lunch was terrible. They ordered a large tea. There was a cold supper. The drinks weren't very cold.

Illnesses

We do not use articles with most illnesses such as diabetes, pneumonia, influenza. Some people still use *the* with such common infectious diseases:

(*the*) flu, (*the*) measles, (*the*) mumps, (*the*) chicken pox
and with the condition (*the*) hiccups.

Some health conditions require the indefinite article *a*:

a cold, *a* temperature, *a* fever, *a* headache.

Names

Many names do not have an article. These names include personal names, geographical names and names connected with certain times of the year. (See Appendix 2 for examples of names that take *the*.)

Personal names

Personal names – a first or Christian name, a surname or both first and surname, with or without a title such as Dr, Mr, Mrs, Miss or Ms – have no article before the names:

Anne Smith
Ms Anne Smith
Dr Anne Smith
Mr Paul Smith
Professor Simon Evans
Miss Anita Peabody
President Kennedy
Captain Lewis
Chief Inspector Johnson

If we use a surname in the plural to refer to a married couple or to a whole family, then we use *the*:

the Smiths (Dr Anne Smith and her husband, Mr Paul Smith, and their children).

Geographical names

No article is used before continents or countries:
> North/South America, Europe, Southeast Asia, Africa.
> Canada, England, Scotland, Australia, Zimbabwe.

The is used with names ending with a compass point:
> *The* Middle East, *The* Southeast, *the* Northwest, etc.

The is sometimes used for a few countries such as *The* Sudan and *The* Lebanon, but this use is less common now (see Appendix 2 for uses of *the* with plural geographical names).

No article is used before cities, lakes and mountains (see Appendix 2 for the use of *the* with mountain ranges):
> London, Penang, Ipoh, Asunción, Naples.
> Lake Michigan, Lake Titicaca, Lake Windermere.
> Everest, Ararat, Mont Blanc.

No article is used before names of streets, buildings, airports, cathedrals, stations, parks:
> Oxford Street, Buckingham Palace, Changi Airport, Canterbury Cathedral,
> Euston Station, Kew Gardens, Park Avenue, Reading Gaol,
> Schipol Airport, St Mary's Church, Waterloo Station, Windsor Safari Park.

Time and dates

We do not use an article when we refer to holidays or festivals, days of the week and months of the year, or years when we want to refer to the period as a time in the calendar:
> Ramadan, Christmas, New Year's Day, Dominion Day, Passover,
> Easter, Chinese New Year, ANZAC Day.
> Monday to Friday, January to December.
> 1702 (seventeen-oh-two), 1814 (eighteen fourteen), 1954 (nineteen fifty-four),
> 1975 (nineteen seventy-five), 1989 (nineteen eighty-nine).

However, when we refer to a ten-year period or a decade, *the* is used with the plural:
> *the* 1900s (*the* nineteen hundreds), *the* 1930s (*the* thirties), *the* 1950s (*the* fifties).

A can be used with days of the week when no particular day is referred to:
> I left Santos on *a* Tuesday.
> You arrive on *a* Wednesday.

Days of the week can have a plural, but months of the year do not have a plural:
> Lots of people hate Mondays.
> The shops are closed on Wednesdays.
> The park is closed in January and February.

Appendix 4
MULTI-WORD VERBS

Multi-word or *phrasal* verbs can be very difficult to learn. This is because there are so many of them and you cannot always understand what they mean even if you understand all the words.

For example, *look up* might mean 'to look up at the sky' but it more often means 'to look for a word in a reference book' or 'to contact someone':

She *looked up* the word 'phrasal' in the dictionary.
When you go to Manila be sure to *look up* my friends.

Multi-word verbs are very common, especially in spoken, informal English.

The following list gives you the meanings of some common multi-word verbs and also gives you some rules for word order for these verbs.

Verb + adverb (without an object)

This is a type of *intransitive* verb and has no object:

The new students are *getting on* very well. (settling down and succeeding in their work)
The Boeing 747 *took off*. (left the ground and flew into the air)
Don't *stay up* too late. (remain out of bed)

Verb + adverb + object

This is a type of *transitive* verb and has an object:

Have you *handed in* your application yet? (submitted)
We can *put up* your cousin for the weekend.
We can *put* your cousin *up* for the weekend.

The object can be either a noun or noun phrase or a pronoun. If the object is a noun or noun phrase, it can come either at the end of the multi-word verb or between the verb and the adverb:

Have you *handed in* your application yet?
Have you *handed* your application *in* yet?

If the object is a pronoun, then it must come between the verb and the adverb:

Have you *handed* it *in* yet?
We can *put* her *up* for the weekend.
They *called* it *off*.

310

Verb + preposition + object

With this type of phrase, the object, whether it is a noun or a pronoun, must come after the preposition:

Some people can't *cope with* very loud music. (accept or endure it)
Anne *looked after* my cat when I was in India. ⎫
Anne *looked after* her/it when I was in India. ⎬ (fed and took care of)

Some common prepositions used in these multi-word verbs are:
across, after, for, into, over, past

Verb + adverb + preposition

These verbs always have a non-literal meaning. Like the previous example, the object always comes after the preposition:

I'm not going to *put up with* his bad temper any longer. (accept or tolerate)
Trish *is looking forward to* getting a good job. ⎫
Trish *is looking forward to* it. ⎬ (anticipating with pleasure)
Women should *stand up for* their rights. ⎫
Women should *stand up for* them. ⎬ (defend and advocate)

Appendix 5
PLURALS OF NOUNS

Regular plurals

Most nouns form the plural by adding -s to singular noun:

book	books
cat	cats
house	houses

(i) Nouns that end in -s, -z, -x, -ch or -sh add -es to the singular noun:

gas	gases
buzz	buzzes
box	boxes
watch	watches
wish	wishes

(ii) Nouns that end in -y:

If the letter before -y is a consonant, change the -y to -i and add -es:

fly	flies
copy	copies

If the letter before -y is a vowel, there is no change; simply add -s:

play	plays
day	days
monkey	monkeys

(iii) Nouns that end in -o:

If the -o is preceded by a vowel, add -s:

bamboo	bamboos
kangaroo	kangaroos
radio	radios
embryo	embryos

If the -o is preceded by a consonant, we usually add -s:

piano	pianos
kilo	kilos

But there are some nouns that add -es. The most common are:

potato	potatoes
tomato	tomatoes
echo	echoes
hero	heroes
veto	vetoes

312

Irregular plurals

(i) Some nouns that end in -f or -fe form the plural by changing the -f to -v and adding -es:

calf	calves
half	halves
knife	knives
leaf	leaves
shelf	shelves
wife	wives

Other nouns ending in -f or -fe have a regular plural:

belief	beliefs
chief	chiefs
cliff	cliffs
proof	proofs
roof	roofs

(ii) There are only seven nouns that change completely:

foot	*feet*
goose	*geese*
tooth	*teeth*
man	*men*
woman	*women*
mouse	*mice*
louse	*lice*

(iii) Two common nouns add -en to form the plural:

child	children
ox	oxen

(iv) Some nouns do not have a different form for the plural:

sheep	*sheep*
deer	*deer*
aircraft	*aircraft*
spacecraft	*spacecraft*

(v) Some nouns from Greek:

Those ending in -is in the singular change to -es in the plural:

analysis	analyses
basis	bases
thesis	theses

Those ending in -on in the singular change to -a in the plural:

criterion	criteria
phenomenon	phenomena

```
┌─────────────────────────────┐
│                             │
│      Appendix 6             │
│    A D J E C T I V E S      │
│    F O L L O W E D   B Y    │
│   P R E P O S I T I O N S   │
│                             │
└─────────────────────────────┘
```

There are no rules to govern the use of prepositions, especially when they follow verbs or adjectives. From the list below you will see that some adjectives can be followed by different prepositions and this affects their meaning and use.

This appendix is a quick reference to the more commonly used adjectives; there are very many more than are listed here and you should refer to a good learners' dictionary. Adjectives which are derived from the past participle form of a verb, such as *surprised*, *interested*, *disappointed*, etc. are not included here and are listed in Unit 4.5.

Adj. + preposition	Example
acceptable to	The contract was *acceptable to* all of those involved.
afraid of	Children are often *afraid of* the dark.
ambitious for	Dick was very *ambitious for* his children.
angry about	Charles was *angry about* the way the matter was handled.
angry with	Jon is very *angry with* Gerry at the moment.
capable of	Tony is very *capable of* forgetting the date of his children's birthdays.
careful of	You should be very *careful of* promising to help.
close to	The castle is very *close to* the railway station.
conscious of	Robert is very *conscious of* the fact that Roger doesn't like him and his work.
dependent on	Sandra is *dependent on* Michael for her job.
different from/to	Pinter's latest play is very *different from/to* his earlier ones.
envious of	Liz is very *envious of* Charles' success.
expert at	The cat was *expert at* getting through its new door.
familiar to	I couldn't remember her name, but her face was very *familiar to* me.
famous for	Scotland is *famous for* its whisky.
fond of	But she's also very *fond of* him.
glad of	Edward was *glad of* the extra money from the trip.
good at	Mary was *good at* persuading people to do things for her.
good for	Eating an apple a day is supposed to be *good for* you.
grateful to	Bobby was very *grateful to* Sheila for lending him the money.
happy with	They were very *happy with* the arrangements that had been made.

314

impatient at	Joan was *impatient at* the thought of having to wait two hours for the plane.
impatient for	Pamela was *impatient for* the film to come on television.
impatient with	Now he is old, Paul gets *impatient with* the children.
important for	It was very *important for* him to be at the meeting.
important to	Although he said nothing during the meeting, it was very *important to* the director that he was present.
independent of	Although he worked at the university, he felt quite *independent of* the department.
innocent of	The captain said he was *innocent of* any negligence.
intent on	Marc is very *intent on* becoming a soldier when he grows up.
jealous of	Roy was very *jealous of* Barry who went on holiday in Senegal.
kind of	It was *kind of* Jim to meet her.
kind to	Elizabeth is very *kind to* animals.
quick at	Lee is very *quick at* understanding the main point of the argument.
similar to	That decision is *similar to* the one we made at our meeting last week.
sorry for	His mother was very *sorry for* him, after he had tried so hard and still failed.
successful in	Keith is very *successful in* his work.

Appendix 7
SPELLING

Nouns

See Appendix 5 for detailed information about plurals.

Verbs

To form the third person singular of the present simple, we follow the same rules as those for the plural form of nouns:

(i) For most verbs, add -s:

look	she looks
write	he writes

(ii) Verbs that end in -s, -z, -x, -ch or -sh add -es to form the third person singular:

pass	he passes
buzz	it buzzes
fax	he faxes
catch	she catches
wash	he washes

(iii) Verbs that end in -y:
If the letter before -y is a consonant, change the -y to -i and add es:

carry	she carries
fly	it flies

If the letter before -y is a vowel, simply add -s:

say	he says
enjoy	she enjoys

(iv) When the verb ends in -o, add -es:

go	it goes
do	he does

When the verb stem ends in -e, we leave out the -e when we add -ed or -ing:

make	making
arrive	they arrived

Adjectives

(i) When the adjective ends in *-e*, we leave out the *-e*, when we form the comparative (*-er*) and superlative (*-est*) (see Units 4.3 and 4.4):

    nice   nic*er*   nic*est*

(ii) To form the comparative and superlative forms (Units 4.3 and 4.4) with adjectives that end in *-y*, we change the *-y* to *-i* and add *-er* or *-est*:

    happy   happ*ier*   happ*iest*

Doubling consonants

When we have a short word with one vowel and one consonant at the end (e.g. hot, scan), we double the consonant before the endings *-er, est, ed* and *ing*:

    hot   hot*ter*   hot*test*
    plan   plan*ned*   plan*ning*

WARNING BOX

We do not do this when a word ends in *-w* or *-y*:

    few   fewer   fewest
    grey   greyer   greyest
    show   showed
    play   played

When the word is longer and the final syllable is stressed, we double the final consonant after a single vowel:

    begin   begin*ning*
    commit   comit*ted*   comit*ting*
    prefer   prefer*red*   prefer*ring*

If the stress is on an earlier syllable, the final consonant is not doubled:

    develop   developed   developing
    profit   profited   profiting

In British English, when a word ends in *-l*, we double the *-l* before an ending even though the stress is on an earlier syllable:

    marvel   marvel*lous* (*British*)
                marvelous (*American*)
    travel   travel*led* (*British*)
                traveled (*American*)

Appendix 8
PUNCTUATION

Capital letters

We use *capital letters* for:

(i) the word at the beginning of a sentence:
   The day began with the sun.
   It was the best of times and the worst of times.

(ii) whenever we use the first person singular 'I':
   I met her at the race-course.
   You and I should be friends.

(iii) with names, days of the week and months:
   Thomas Hardy
   The Times
   Mount Everest
   Monday
   August.

Full stop

We put a *full stop* at the end of sentences which are statements (see Unit 1.1) or imperatives (see Units 1.4 and 1.5):
   He listened to the sound of the storm.

Comma

We use a *comma* when:

(i) we are dividing two main clauses joined by *and, or, but* when the subject (see Unit 1.1) is different in each clause:
   She came in and closed the door. (no comma, subject is the same in each clause)
   The sky was blue, and the sun shone brightly. (comma, subject is different in each clause)

(ii) after a subordinate clause but not before:
   When he came home, he felt very angry.
   He felt very angry when he came home.

318

(iii) around a relative clause which gives additional information (see Unit 4.14):
Alfred Hitchcock, who made 'Psycho', was an Englishman.

(iv) after an adverbial (see Units 4.6 and 4.7), but not before:
On Saturday, they went to the park.
They went to the park on Saturday.

(v) around linking words:
It's raining now. We shall, however, go out for walk.

INDEX

320

ANSWER KEY

UNIT 1.1 WORD ORDER: STATEMENTS Form

TASK ONE

	Subject	Verb	Complement	Direct object	Indirect object	Adverbial
(a)	He	woke up				early
(b)	Edward Young	wrote		novels		
(c)	The Queen	gave		a medal	the captain	
(d)	Elizabeth	became	Queen			in 1952
(e)	She	seemed	very ill			that day
(f)	The light	went out				
(g)	The dog	bit		the postman		
(h)	Mr Blandings	builds		his dream house		
(i)	Romeo	loved		Juliet		
(j)	Doug	taught		English	Andrea	

TASK TWO

(a) She is coming next week.
(b) The boy won a prize./A boy won the prize.
(c) She gave him a kiss.
(d) The young boy blushed.
(e) The man was ill.
(f) He became tired easily./He easily became tired.
(g) The girl disobeyed her father.

(h) She was walking with the dustman.
(i) Diane gave him the money for the beer.
(j) He liked her.

UNIT 1.2 QUESTIONS Form

TASK ONE

In some of the statements or questions there is more than one possible answer. The two possible answers are put with / between them.
(a) Who
(b) Why
(c) Where/When
(d) Why
(e) How/Why
(f) Where
(g) Who
(h) What
(i) How/Why
(j) When

TASK TWO

These are only suggested answers. There are other things you could say.
(a) What are you going to buy in Manila?
(b) Where did he get his shirt?
(c) Why are you sitting there?
(d) When are we going to Singapore?
(e) What did they bring to the party?
(f) Where did she find that book?
(g) What did you read on the train?
(h) How did he jump over the fence?
(i) What did you ask the teacher?
(j) Who lives in that house?

UNIT 1.3 QUESTIONS Function

TASK THREE

There are many possible answers. The ones below are only suggestions.
(a) What do you do?
(b) What can I do for you?
(c) Who is it?

(d) What is it?
(e) How come you didn't meet me last night?
(f) Who knows?
(g) How about going to the new play? *or*
     Why not go to the new play?

UNIT 1.4 WORD ORDER: IMPERATIVES Form

TASK ONE

Some suggestions:
Stand on the right; get up; don't touch the painting; get to bed early; look out; do the work tonight; don't jump over the fence; drive slowly; walk slowly; don't stay out late.

TASK TWO

(a) Get up
(b) Walk slowly
(c) Look out
(d) Don't jump over the fence
(e) Stand on the right
(f) Don't touch the painting
(g) Drive slowly
(h) Do the work tonight
(i) Get to bed early
(j) Don't stay out late

UNIT 1.5 WORD ORDER: IMPERATIVES Function

TASK ONE

(a) Instruction
(b) Request
(c) Invitation
(d) Warning/Advice
(e) Warning

TASK THREE

(a) Put your foot down!
(b) Get cracking!
(c) Come down to earth!

UNIT 1.6 ADVERBS OF FREQUENCY Form and function

TASK ONE

The adverbs here are only suggestions. Others may be used, but they should be put in the same position in the sentence.

(a) John will **soon** be here.
(b) Do you **always/often/usually/ever**/etc. go to Italy for your holidays?
(c) Charles Dickens **never** forgot his poor childhood.
(d) The milkman **always/usually** calls on Monday for his money.
(e) I've **never/already** seen that film.
(f) I will **always** remember you.
(g) Lions **never** attack people first.
(h) The prince **always/never/sometimes/rarely/usually/seldom/often** etc. had dinner with his wife.
(i) Europe will **soon**/etc. be united.
(j) Have you **ever** tried to swim across the channel?

UNIT 2.1 BE, HAVE: PRESENT SIMPLE Form

TASK ONE

(a) are; have; are; have; are; have; have; are
(b) *The 'Babar' books are still being published so you should use the present simple form. However, if you are thinking about when the books were written in 1931, it would be possible to use the past simple form. The last blank must be **is** because it refers to now.*
    is/was; is/was; has/had; is/was; has/had; is/was; have/had; is.
(c) is; is; is.
(d) is; is; is; is; has; is.

TASK TWO

are; are; have; have; are; have; are; have; are; are; have; are; are; are; are; have; are.

UNIT 2.2 BE, HAVE: PRESENT SIMPLE Function

TASK ONE

Suggested answers:
(a) She hasn't got £20. Her daughter has some money. The shoes are too small. 'Do you have size 10?'

(b) The lady has a cold. 'Where is the jam?' The baby has the jam. The baby is under the table. The cat has four kittens. The cat is in the corner.
(c) 'It is a big house. It has four bedrooms. It has three bathrooms. It has a large garden.'

UNIT 2.3 BE AND HAVE: SIMPLE PAST Form

TASK ONE

was; were; had; had; were.

TASK TWO

was; was; was; was; was; was; had.
was; was; had; did not have; had.

UNIT 2.5 PRESENT SIMPLE Form

TASK ONE

I eat You eat He eats She eats It eats	We eat They eat	I drink You drink He drinks She drinks It drinks	We drink They drink

TASK THREE

carry; weigh; measure; record; measures.

make; holds; moves; gets; means; displaces; puts.

UNIT 2.6 PRESENT SIMPLE Function

TASK THREE

(a) 'There goes our bus!'
(b) 'It's not the end of the world. You have another one at home.'
(c) 'Here comes a taxi.'
(d) 'That name rings a bell. I think I know her.'

ANSWER KEY

UNIT 2.7 PRESENT CONTINUOUS Form

TASK ONE

are smoking; are drinking; is eating; is skipping; are exercising; are reading; are paying.

TASK THREE

Student B: No, he's writing a letter.
Student C: No, she's thinking about skiing.
Student D: No, he's drawing a cartoon.
Student E: No, she's painting her fingernails.
Student F: No, he's writing a shopping list.
Student G: No, she's setting/fixing her watch.
Student H: No, he's talking to his friend.
Student I: No, she's doing a maths problem.

UNIT 2.8 PRESENT CONTINUOUS Function

TASK THREE

(a) How's it going?
     How are you getting on?
     How are you doing?

(b) What's going on?

(c) I'm hoping for the best.

(d) He/She's sitting on the fence.

UNIT 2.9 PAST SIMPLE Form

TASK ONE

(a)

Stem	Past	Stem	Past
add	*added*	leave	*left*
become	*became*	like	*liked*
begin	*began*	live	*lived*
break	*broke*	love	*loved*
bring	*brought*	make	*made*
carry	*carried*	mean	*meant*
choose	*chose*	need	*needed*
come	*came*	play	*played*
decrease	*decreased*	put	*put*
do	*did*	read	*read*
drink	*drank*	say	*said*
drive	*drove*	see	*saw*
eat	*ate*	send	*sent*
fall	*fell*	speak	*spoke*
find	*found*	take	*took*
get	*got*	teach	*taught*
go	*went*	think	*thought*
hold	*held*	travel	*travelled*
keep	*kept*	understand	*understood*
know	*knew*	want	*wanted*
laugh	*laughed*	write	*wrote*

(b)   There are eleven regular verbs in the list.

TASK TWO
made; found; meant; demonstrated; painted; blew; grew.

TASK THREE
left; went; left; put; arrived; went; found; moved; entered; started.

UNIT 2.10 PAST SIMPLE Function

TASK THREE

(a) What did I tell you?
(b) Whatever possessed you to do that?

UNIT 2.11 PAST CONTINUOUS Form

TASK ONE

were wearing; were wearing; were ordering; (were) making; were speaking; were ordering.
was getting; were laughing; (were) enjoying.
was he getting angry; was not ordering.

TASK TWO

was travelling; were taking; were working; were painting; was spending; was walking; was having; was doing; was sticking; waving; rolling.

UNIT 2.12 PAST CONTINUOUS Function

TASK ONE

were you doing; was photocopying; were you working; were you doing; was stamping; were you doing; was using; were you doing; was getting; was copying; were you doing; was writing; (was) telephoning; were you working; was looking; was kicking; wasn't working; was adjusting; was not looking; was typing; was looking up; was making.

UNIT 2.14 FUTURE: WILL, SHALL + STEM Form

TASK ONE

*Your answers may be different because you have put 'Yes' or 'No' in different answers. But as long as you have the correct pronoun and **will** with 'Yes' and **won't** with 'No' then your answers will also be correct.*
(a) Yes, I will.
(b) No, it won't.
(c) Yes, they will.

(d) No, there won't.
(e) Yes, you will.
(f) Yes, they will.
(g) No, they won't.
(h) Yes, she will.
(i) No, he won't.
(j) Yes, you will.

TASK TWO

(a) Will they finish before 6 o'clock?
(b) Will you see Margaret and Carole?
(c) Will they catch the early train?
(d) Will she sit at the front of the bus?
(e) Will they find a cure for cancer?
(f) Will we finish the experiment?
(g) Will they use more than two tins of paint?
(h) Will Real Madrid win the match?
(i) Will air travel be cheaper in the future?
(j) Will the government increase taxes?

TASK THREE

(a) Yes, they will.
(b) Yes, I will.
(c) No, they won't.
(d) No, she (probably) won't.
(e) Yes, they will.
(f) Yes, we (probably) will.
(g) No, they (probably) won't.
(h) I don't know if they will.
(i) Yes, I think it will.
(j) Yes, they/it will.

UNIT 2.15 FUTURE: WILL/SHALL + STEM Function

TASK TWO

These are suggested answers. You do not have to say exactly the same thing to be correct.
(a) Shall I help you./ Shall I carry that for you?
(b) I'll get/reach that for you.
(c) I'll help you paint the flat.
(d) Shall I do that for you?
(e) Shall I telephone the garage?

(f) I'll buy you a cup of coffee.
(g) Shall I get it down?
(h) I'll look after the children for you.
(i) Shall I help you?
(j) I'll find your Mummy and Daddy.

TASK THREE

These are suggested answers.
(a) I'll have lunch now.
(b) I'll type it for you.
(c) Yes, they will play their music too loud.
(d) Will you shut up!
(e) I'll help you.

UNIT 2.16 FUTURE: BE + GOING TO + STEM Form

TASK ONE

These are not the only possible answers. Your answers will be different but they should follow the same pattern.
(a) Yes, I am/I'm going to do it tonight.
(b) No, she isn't. She's going to buy a typewriter.
(c) I don't know if they are.
(d) Yes, they are.
(e) No, we aren't.
(f) No, I'm not.
(g) Yes, it is.
(h) I don't know if they are.
(i) Yes, she/it is.
(j) Yes, she is.

TASK TWO

These are suggested questions.
(a) Are you going to finish that book?
(b) Is it going to rain?
(c) Is he going to buy a computer?
(d) Is she going to (go to) the concert?
(e) Are they going to have a party?
(f) Is she going to buy a coat?
(g) Are they going to (go to) the cinema?
(h) Are you going (to go) for a walk?
(i) Are you going to buy that car?
(j) Are you going to bake the bread yourself?

UNIT 2.17 FUTURE: BE + GOING TO + STEM Function

TASK ONE

(a) I'm not going to continue; I'm going to start.
(b) are (you) going to do; I'm going to learn to speak; I'm going to learn to play; I'm going to move; I'm going to ride; I'm going to play.

TASK TWO

What is Paul going to do next year? He's going to buy a Rolls Royce.
What is John going to do in 1993? He's going to build a house.
What is Cathy going to do next winter? She's going to go skiing in the Alps.
What is Pete going to do next summer? He's going to visit Paris.
What is Linda going to do in June? She's going to get married.

UNIT 2.18 FUTURE: PRESENT SIMPLE Form and function

TASK ONE

(a) have
(b) arrives
(c) am
(d) starts
(e) leave
(f) is
(g) is
(h) starts; end
(i) finish
(j) is

UNIT 2.19 FUTURE: PRESENT CONTINUOUS Form and function

TASK ONE

(a) is buying
(b) is flying
(c) are you doing; am playing
(d) is meeting

(e) are moving
(f) is going
(g) is playing
(h) are getting
(i) are announcing
(j) are having; is bringing; are arriving; are eating

UNIT 2.20 PRESENT PERFECT Form

TASK ONE

Positive	Negative	Questions
(a) have seen	haven't seen	have you seen?
(b) have been	haven't been	have they been?
(c) has gone	hasn't gone	has she gone?
(d) has rained	hasn't rained	has it rained?
(e) have run	haven't run	have you run?
(f) have waited	haven't waited	have we waited?
(g) has played	hasn't played	has he played?
(h) have wanted	haven't wanted	have I wanted?
(i) have walked	haven't walked	have they walked?
(j) has had	hasn't had	has she had?
(k) have stayed	haven't stayed	have you stayed?
(l) have thought	haven't thought	have I thought?
(m) has sold	haven't sold	have we sold?
(n) has sung	hasn't sung	has she sung?
(o) has won	hasn't won	has she won?

TASK TWO

(a) have not been; has gone
(b) has lived; has decided
(c) has written; has won
(d) has become
(e) has changed; have had
(f) has sold
(g) has lived; have settled
(h) have studied; have lived
(i) have helped
(j) have learnt/learned

UNIT 2.21 PRESENT PERFECT Function

TASK ONE

(a) have made; have returned; have never forgotten; have been; have visited; have been; have never been.
(b) has also called; has received; has become; have started; has made; has travelled.
(c) have existed; have drifted; have affected; has been.

UNITS 2.22 and 2.23 USED TO Form and function

TASK ONE

(a) She used to play badminton but now she plays tennis.
(b) She used to go swimming but now she prefers skiing.
(c) She used to read historical novels but now she reads biographies.
(d) She used to go to the cinema often but now she usually stays home and watches videos.
(e) She used to sit for exams but now she sets exams for her students.
(f) She used to speak French all the time but now she speaks English.
(g) She used to collect stamps but now she doesn't collect anything.
(h) She used to think she wanted to be a business executive but now she is a university lecturer.
(i) She used to plan to live in Belgium but now she lives in Canada.
(j) She never used to like travelling but now she goes on many trips.

UNIT 2.24 PASSIVE Form

TASK ONE

(a) Raymond was seen by Fred at the theatre.
(b) Many of the houses were destroyed by the storm.
(c) Cars are going to be sold in that showroom.
(d) The horse's reins were held by Juliet.
(e) A film was made of Mozart's life./A film of Mozart's life was made.
(f) 'Brighton Rock' was written by Graham Greene.
(g) The President was met by the Prime Minister in the Bahamas.
(h) India was ruled by the British for 200 years.
(i) Fawkes was executed for treason.
(j) Their grandmother was given flowers by the young visitors on her birthday./Flowers were given to their grandmother by the young visitors on her birthday.

TASK TWO

(a) The ship was seen.
(b) The cow was milked at dawn.
(c) The man was hit by the car.
(d) 'Macbeth' was written by Shakespeare.
(e) The jewels were stolen.

UNIT 2.25 PASSIVE Function

TASK ONE

(a) The 'Sot-weed Factor' was written by Barth.
(b) The teacher says/said prayers.
(c) The house was painted by the old man.
(d) The little girl broke the window.
(e) Gillow made those chairs.
(f) Walt Disney created Mickey Mouse.
(g) The weather forecast was given by Frank.
(h) Romeo loved Juliet./Romeo was loved by Juliet.
(i) The Queen was met by the captain./The Queen met the captain.
(j) Margaret was elected by the people.

TASK TWO

The book was written by Philip early in 1989. It was liked by the public and it became a bestseller. Philip was asked by his publishers to write a sequel. The sequel would be published a year later. Philip was frightened by all this. He didn't think he could work that fast and he had no ideas. But his wife thought it was a good idea. He was encouraged by her to sign the contract.

UNIT 2.27 MODAL VERBS Form

TASK ONE

Central	Marginal	Semi-auxiliary
(a), (c), (e), (f), (g), (i), (j)	(b)	(d), (h)

UNIT 2.28 MODALS Function

TASK ONE

IMPORTANT TO DO	(a), (d), (f), (h)
IMPORTANT NOT TO DO	(g)
NECESSARY TO DO	(e), (f), (h), (j)
NOT NECESSARY TO DO	(b), (i)
CERTAIN ABOUT SOMETHING	(c)

TASK TWO

October 4th: I must go to the bank and I must arrange a loan.
I haven't got any biscuits; I need to buy some.
I mustn't water the plants – too much water kills them.
It's Mary's birthday; I mustn't forget the theatre tickets.

October 10th: I must/need to take the car to the garage for a service.
I must send Robert the money I owe him.
I mustn't/don't need to tell Jane about the holiday with Mary.
The kitchen light's broken; I must buy new fixture.

TASK THREE

(a) Needs must! (b) You must be joking. (c) He must be joking.

UNIT 2.29 CAN, COULD Function

TASK TWO

(a) Can/Could you come to dinner next week?
(b) You can/could have a lovely holiday in Jamaica.
(c) You can/could earn a lot of money in that job.
(d) The value of your shares can/could go up or down.
(e) Can't/Couldn't you go faster?
(f) She can swim across that river.

339

TASK FOUR

(a) Could be.
(b) You can't be serious!
(c) I couldn't say.

UNIT 2.30 MAY/MIGHT Function

TASK ONE

(a) 'We may go to New York for our holidays,' John always said to people who asked him about holidays. 'Then again we may not.' People were always confused. (**Future possibility**)

(b) DANIEL: I'd like to take Joanne to the beach today. May I borrow the car, Mum? (**Polite request**)
   MOTHER: You only passed your test two weeks ago.
   DANIEL: Well, I did pass it.
   MOTHER: It's a long way to go. You might get tired. You haven't driven that far before. (**Future possibility**)
   DANIEL: I won't. I'll drive carefully. Please.
   MOTHER: Then don't be late back.
   DANIEL: Of course not. May I borrow the car then? (**Polite request**)
   MOTHER: Yes, you may. (**Giving permission**)

(c) LEN: It's a good film.
   PHIL: Yes, and it'll be crowded. We may not get in. (**Future possibility**)
   LEN: We might, if we get there early. (**Future possibility**)
   PHIL: But I want to finish this essay first. May I? (**Polite request**)
   LEN: No, you may not. Do that tomorrow. Let's go to see the film now. (**Refusing permission**)

TASK TWO

(a) 'We could go to New York for our holidays,' John always said to people who asked him about holidays. 'Then again we *may* not.' People were always confused.

(b) DANIEL: I'd like to take Joanne to the beach today. Can/Could I borrow the car, Mum?
   MOTHER: You only passed your test two weeks ago.
   DANIEL: Well, I did pass it.
   MOTHER: It's a long way to go. You could get tired. You haven't driven that far before.
   DANIEL: I won't. I'll drive carefully. Please.
   MOTHER: Then don't be late back!

DANIEL: Of course not. <u>Can/Could</u> I borrow the car then?
MOTHER: Yes, you <u>can</u>.

(c) LEN: It's a good film.
    PHIL: Yes, and it'll be crowded. We *may* not get in.
    LEN: We *might*, if we get there early.
    PHIL: But I want to finish this essay first. <u>Can/Could</u> I?
    LEN: No, you <u>can't</u>. Do that tomorrow. Let's go to see the film now.

TASK THREE

(a) I might have known/I might have guessed.
(b) Maybe.

UNIT 2.31 SHOULD, OUGHT TO Function

TASK ONE

IMPORTANT TO DO	(b), (g), (h)
BETTER TO DO OR TO HAVE	(c), (i)
GIVE ADVICE OR AN OPINION	(a), (e)
ALMOST CERTAIN	(d), (f), (j)

TASK TWO

(a) You should lose weight.
(b) You should drive carefully.
(c) You should get up earlier.
(d) You shouldn't stay up so late.
(e) You should give up smoking.

TASK THREE

(a) How should I know?
(b) Why should I?

UNIT 2.32 WILL, SHALL Function

TASK ONE

GENERAL TRUTH	(a), (i)
ASKING ABOUT THE FUTURE	(f), (j)
PREDICTION	(b), (g)
REQUEST	(c), (h)
SUGGESTION	(d), (e)

UNIT 2.33 WOULD Function

TASK ONE

(a) Would you give me some money for food, please?
(b) Would you be quiet, please, I'm trying to work.
(c) Would you mind helping me get to a garage?
(d) Would you turn off the radio, please?
(e) Would you mind if I bring a friend with me?
(f) Would you mind if I left early?
(g) Would you look after the children until seven o'clock?
(h) Would you ask George to wait for me?
(i) Would you answer the phone, please?
(j) Would you make some tea, please?

TASK TWO

Possible answers:
(a) A: Would you help me put up this tent?
      B: Certainly./Yes, of course.
(b) A: Would you mind taking this letter to the Post Office for me?
      B: No, of course not.
(c) A: Would you mind not playing that guitar so loud?
      B: I'm sorry. I'll be quieter.
(d) A: Would you let me paint your picture?
      B: Certainly. It'll be a pleasure.
(e) A: Would you mind taking a photograph of us?
      B: Certainly./Of course.

UNIT 2.34 CONDITIONAL: POSSIBLE Form

TASK ONE

There are other possible answers. These are suggestions.
(a) If you see the bear, you mustn't be afraid.
(b) If you come home late, there'll be no food left.
(c) If the house fell down, we'd be all right.
(d) If you see him coming, you must tell mother.
(e) If you saw him in the morning, he would always be angry.
(f) If the train's late, he won't be here until after midnight.
(g) If she was ill, he would always worry.
(h) If you go early, you'll find a lot of bargains.
(i) If the exam is easy, you'll be successful.
(j) If they like it, they'll buy it.

TASK TWO

(a) *These will vary according to your choices; but for the answers given, the types are as below.*

Type A	Type B	Type C
(a), (b), (d), (f), (h), (i), (j)		(c), (e), (g)

(b)
Come home late and there'll be no food left. (b)
Go early and you'll find a lot of bargains. (h)
Work hard and you'll be successful. (i)

UNIT 2.35 CONDITIONAL: POSSIBLE Function

TASK ONE

Habit	(b)
Future certainties	(a), (f), (g), (i), (j)
Future possibilities	(h)
Advice	(c), (e)
Suggestions	
Facts	(d)

TASK THREE

(a) *Jane:* Do you think they'll decide to change the directors?
You: It's a bit iffy.

(b) *Jim:* If you're suggesting that I was responsible for losing that money . . .
You: Not at all, but if the cap fits, wear it.

UNIT 2.36 CONDITIONAL: IMPOSSIBLE Form

TASK ONE

(a) If John **was/were** in Venice, he could see the carnival now.
(b) If it **was raining**, we **would go** to the cinema.
(c) If you **had** a video, you could record the film.
(d) If Anna hadn't got married, she **would enter** for the Miss World competition.
(e) If Sammy **had gone** to the gym regularly, he would have won the Mr Hot Bod competition.
(f) If you **had** an invitation, you could go to the party.
(g) If you **drove**, we could hire a car for the holiday.
(h) If you were younger, you **would enjoy** rock music.
(i) If Mavis **was/were** rich, she would travel by Concorde.
(j) If it was a funny film, I **would go and see** it.

TASK TWO

Here are some suggestions. You may have others.
(a) If I was a rich man, I'd help the poor.
(b) If Japan were nearer, I'd go there more often.
(c) If you read 'The Times', you'd be better informed.
(d) If pigs could fly, they would look very funny.
(e) If the wind blew strongly, the windows would break.
(f) If I crashed his car, my dad would be very angry.
(g) If he had millions, he'd make a great film.
(h) If she had talent, she'd be a big star.
(i) If she really loved you, she'd forgive you.
(j) If you thought about it, you wouldn't go.

UNIT 2.37 CONDITIONAL: IMPOSSIBLE Function

TASK ONE

These answers are suggestions.
(a) If she had her paints with her, she would paint it.
(b) If he had his camera, he would photograph it.
(c) If he had his gun, he would shoot it.
(d) If he caught it, he would put it in a cage.
(e) If she had a pen, she would write about it.

UNIT 2.38 CONDITIONAL: WISHING Form and function

TASK ONE

(a) He wishes he could travel round the world in a yacht.
(b) She wishes the disco near her house would close.
(c) They wish they had a very big house in the country.
(d) She wishes it would rain on Sunday.
(e) He wishes he could spend all his time in a library reading and studying.
(f) I wish I was a famous dancer.
(g) He wishes he could ride a horse like a cowboy.
(h) She wishes she ran a big company.
(i) He wishes he could live his schooldays again and work harder.
(j) I wish I could fly like a bird.

TASK TWO

Suggested answers:
(a) I wish I was at home.
(b) I wish I had a gun.
(c) I wish I could run very fast.
(d) I wish they were small cats.
(e) I wish we had some food for them.

UNIT 2.39 INDIRECT SPEECH: STATEMENTS Form

TASK ONE

There are several variations here. The first four show alternative forms which can be used in the rest.
(a) Bob Bruce says that he saw her driving to Bristol on Wednesday.
   Bob Bruce said that he saw her driving to Bristol on Wednesday.
(b) Donna Wallace says that she's gone to see her mother in Australia.
   Donna Wallace said that she went to see her mother in Australia.
(c) Joe Burgess says she's getting married again.
   Joe Burgess said she's getting married again.
(d) Daisy Runcorn says her first husband has come back.
   Daisy Runcorn said her first husband has come back.
(e) Phil Read says he never liked her. She's gone and he's glad.
(f) Rita Golding said she had an accident.
(g) Norman Enright says she's in a hospital near Chelmsford.
(h) Ed Young says she's bought a mansion in Switzerland.
(i) Al Reynolds said the tax people wanted her.
(j) Maggy May says her son is ill.

UNIT 2.40 INDIRECT SPEECH: QUESTIONS, REQUESTS, IMPERATIVES Form

TASK ONE

(a) The reporter on the 'Daily Stag' asked her if she is/was going to marry Jim Randy.
(b) The reporter on the 'Telegram' asked her when she would/will make her next film.
(c) The reporter on the 'Protector' asked her why she left Apex Films.
(d) The reporter on the 'Daily Stun' asked her how much she was paid for her last picture.
(e) The reporter on the 'Daily Wail' asked her where she is/was going for her honeymoon.
(f) The reporter on the 'Daily Excess' asked her to give them a photograph of her new luxury home.

(g) The reporter on the 'Tomes' asked if she has/had to make a picture with David Rabbit, or if she can/could break that contract.
(h) The reporter on the 'Daily Winner' asked her to stand by the window for a photograph.
(i) The reporter on 'Tonight' asked her how her children are/were now.
(j) The reporter on the 'Post' asked her if she has read the script for her new film yet.

TASK TWO

The reporter asked him . . .
He was asked . . .
   what he likes/liked most about the Swedes.
   what he dislikes/disliked most about them.
   what he most respects/respected about the Swedes.
   what Swedish characteristics or activities disgust/disgusted him.
   what he thinks/thought of Swedish women.
   what his impression is/was of Swedish politics.
   what his impression is/was of Swedish television.
   what he thinks/thought of the sense of humour.
   what he thinks/thought is the favourite hobby of the Swedes.
   in what way Sweden is/was better than Britain.

UNIT 2.41 INDIRECT SPEECH Function

TASK ONE

A possible report:

The interviewer asked Julian Critchley what his idea of perfect happiness was/is. He replied that it was/is love after an early supper from Fortnum & Mason.
He was then asked what his greatest fear was/is and he said that is was/is suffocation.
Then the interviewer asked him which historical figure he most identified with and he said that it was the Rev. Sidney Smith, because he was too good a Christian to take religion seriously.
He was then asked which living person he most admires. He answered that it is Sir Fitzroy Maclean who is a brave soldier, skilful diplomat and brilliant author.
The reporter then asked him which trait he most deplores in himself and he told her it is selfishness.
When she asked which trait he most deplores in others, he said it is tactlessness – other people telling him that he is selfish.
He was asked which vehicles he owned. He said it was a Rover 827.
She then asked him what his greatest extravagance is and he told her he has two – collecting Staffordshire pottery and his daughters' weddings.
When she asked him which objects he always carries with him, he said they are a pen, Veganin, a comb and a Barclays Gold Card.

He was then asked what makes him most depressed and he said that it is feeling below par.

Then he was asked what he most disliked about his appearance and he said that it is his double chin.

She asked him what his most unappealing habit was. He said that it was making jokes at Mrs T's expense.

She asked him what his favourite smell is and he told her it is ripe Ogen melons.

Then he was asked what his favourite word is and he said it is Emerald.

Then he was asked what his favourite building is and he said it is the Gatehouse at Stokesay Castle.

She then asked him what his favourite journey is and he told her that it is Ludlow to Shrewsbury and back via Bishop's Castle in early summer.

When she asked him what or who is the greatest love in his life, he said it is South Shropshire.

When she asked what he considers the most overrated virtue, he said it is chastity.

He was asked on what occasions he lied and he said it was when he had to save himself and others from embarrassment.

She asked him which words and phrases he most over uses, and he said it is the word 'Right'.

When he was asked what his greatest regret was, he said that it was that he was never appointed Assistant Postmaster-General.

He was asked when and where he was happiest. He said it was in 1950–1951 in Paris when he was a student in love and had a monthly allowance of £30.

He was asked how he relaxes and he said he sleeps after lunch and reads novels.

When she asked him what single thing would improve the quality of his life, he said it was the remarriage of his first wife.

He was asked which talent he would most like to have and he said it was to be able to play the clarinet (jazz) and read poetry.

She asked him what his motto would be and he told her it would be 'Roll with the punches'.

She asked him what keeps him awake at night and he said it is stomach ache.

When she asked him how he would like to die, he said swiftly in a good restaurant but before the presentation of the bill.

Finally, she asked him how he would like to be remembered. He said he would like to be remembered by a line on a tombstone in Wistanstowe churchyard: 'I told you I was ill'.

UNIT 3.2 ARTICLES: A, AN Form

TASK ONE

an accident	an hour	an experiment
an entertaining film	a horoscope	a hot meal
an example	a heavy machine	an electric current
a union	a new book	a funny cartoon

348

TASK TWO

(a) homework
(b) exercises; tasks; projects
(c) equipment
(d) technicians; experiments
(e) tourists; scenery; sunsets
(f) information; holidays; brochures.

UNIT 3.3 ARTICLES: A, AN Function

TASK ONE

(a) An; an; an; a; an; a; an.
(b) A; a; a; a; an; an; a; a.

TASK TWO

Per/Every	One
	a newspaper
a day	
a thousand	a paper
	a kilo
a year	
a year	a computer
	a computer
	a computer
a year	

UNIT 3.4 ARTICLES: THE Function

TASK ONE

0; 0 *or* the; 0; 0; 0; a; 0 *or* a; the
A *or* The; a; the; 0 *or* the; 0; 0; The *or* A; a; 0; The; the; the; the.
The; a; the *or* a; 0; a.

TASK TWO

the; the; 0; 0; 0; the; the; the; the *or* 0; the/a; the; 0 *or* the; 0.

UNIT 3.5 DETERMINERS: QUANTITY Form

TASK ONE

(a) many books; much milk; many children; many cars; many cows; much coffee; much cake; much rice; much news; much equipment; much food; many chairs; many people; many bicycles; much ice-cream; much tea; much sugar; many carrots; much information; much work.

(b)
There aren't	**There isn't**
many books	much milk
many children	much coffee
many cars	much cake
many cows	much rice
many chairs	much news
many people	much equipment
many bicycles	much food
many carrots	much ice-cream
	much tea
	much sugar
	much information
	much work

TASK TWO

(a) some
(b) some
(c) any; some
(d) some
(e) some; some; any
(f) any

TASK THREE

(a) more; many
(b) Most; all; all; more
(c) Most; many
(d) Most; less; more
(e) fewer

UNIT 3.6 DETERMINERS: QUANTITY Function

TASK ONE

These are the quantity determiners the original writers used. Yours may be different but they may still be correct.

(a) Few
(b) Many
(c) first; more
(d) first; any; few
(e) All
(f) Every
(g) Most
(h) Each; last
(i) first; any
(j) Few
(k) Little
(l) Most; little

TASK FOUR

(a) 'I can do that *in no time.*'
(b) 'There's *no need to worry.* There's *no doubt* you'll get the job.'
(c) '. . . there's *no way* I can finish this in time/go out for the weekend.'
(d) 'This is *no time to say* that/to change your mind/to change the whole plan.'
(e) 'It's *no trouble.'/'*It won't be *any trouble.*'
(f) '*Many happy returns (of the day).*'

UNIT 3.7 DETERMINERS: POSSESSIVES Form and function

TASK ONE

(a) their; their
(b) His; her; His; his; His; his; their
(c) their; its
(d) their; their; their; their; their

TASK THREE

(a) I'd rather do it my way.
(b) It's your turn.
(c) Mind your own business!

UNIT 3.8 DETERMINERS: DEMONSTRATIVES Form and function

TASK ONE

(a) This; these; those; this
(b) These *or* Those; this
(c) Those; these *or* those; this; these
(d) this; This; these

UNIT 3.9 *WH-* DETERMINERS Form and function

TASK ONE

(a) What
(b) Which
(c) What
(d) Whose
(e) Which *or* What
(f) What
(g) Which *or* What
(h) What
(i) What *or* Which
(j) Which

UNIT 4.1 ADJECTIVES Form

TASK ONE

(a) Jess's car is small and green.
(b) The girl was clever and young.
(c) The book was long and boring.
(d) That part of the country is cold and wet.
(e) Juliet's three children are lively and imaginative.

TASK TWO

When I got on board the **modern** ship, I looked at my fellow travellers and tried to guess who they were. There was a **young** couple, a **tall**, **handsome** man with a **shy**, **pretty** girl. They were on their honeymoon. Then I saw a **strong** man walking towards me. He was the ship's sportsman. Every **sunny** morning before breakfast, he ran round the **warm** deck in his **bright** shorts. Further along the deck there was the **old** couple from the cabin next to mine. I guessed the man was a **retired** vicar with his **charming** wife. These were my companions for the next few weeks. When I met them that night, I was wrong about all of them.

UNIT 4.2 ADJECTIVES Function

TASK THREE

(a) blue
(b) green
(c) green
(d) black and blue
(e) yellow

UNIT 4.3 ADJECTIVES: COMPARISON Form

TASK ONE

Positive	Comparative	Superlative
hot	hotter	hottest
cold	colder	coldest
dangerous	more dangerous	most dangerous
bad	worse	worst
lucky	luckier	luckiest
large	larger	largest
comfortable	more comfortable	most comfortable
pleasant	more pleasant	most pleasant
happy	happier	happiest
little	less	least
young	younger	youngest
thick	thicker	thickest
thin	thinner	thinnest
lovely	lovelier	loveliest
important	more important	most important

UNIT 4.4 ADJECTIVES: COMPARISON Function

TASK ONE

Product	Weight	Height	Price	Weather-resistant
Gardenguard	2 kgs	20 cms	£10	very poor
Gnomeland	4 kgs	1 metre	£15	good
Littlemen	1.5 kgs	15 cms	£12	poor
Majorette	3 kgs	25 cms	£17	very good
Rosepixie	5 kgs	15 cms	£30	good
Wonderland	2.5 kgs	10 cms	£20	very good

TASK TWO

We found six makes for our 'best-buy' category. The **cheapest** of these was Enclose, the **most expensive** was Fight. It cost £12.86. Wallsafe was also expensive, but it was the **largest** and one of the **best**. Fight was the **most** effective. Keepoff cost **less** than Wallsafe per litre and was just as effective.

TASK FOUR

(a) As good as gold.
(b) As soon as possible.
(c) The more the merrier.

UNIT 4.5 ADJECTIVES ENDING IN *-ING*, *-ED* Form and function

TASK ONE

Suggested answers:
(a) Burgess writes **interesting** books.
(b) Alice was **amazed** at the way Bix played jazz.
(c) The athlete was very **tired** after running the marathon.

355

(d) A very **bored** Juliet left the dull party early.
(e) The end of the film was **surprising**.
(f) For a small child, a large playful dog might be **frightening**.
(g) The **worried** mother went to the police about her lost child.
(h) The speaker was met by a group of very **interested** people who wanted to hear what he had to say.
(i) Cher arrived at the party wearing an **amazing** dress.
(j) Larsen draws very **amusing** cartoons.

UNIT 4.6 ADVERBS AND ADVERBIALS Form

TASK ONE

(a) The tennis star competed fiercely.
(b) That baby smiles in a lovely way.
(c) Professor Mo lectures badly.
(d) He plays football well.
(e) That book tells the story well.
(f) She behaved very strangely.
(g) He speaks loudly.
(h) They made the film beautifully.
(i) She works hard.
(j) The cat behaves in a friendly way.

UNIT 4.7 ADVERBS AND ADVERBIALS Function

TASK ONE

Possible answers:
(a) The came *at four o'clock*.
(b) Joanne spoke *clearly*.
(c) Martyn was standing *at the door*.
(d) The horse ran *well* in the race.
(e) The young man went to see the old lady *every week*.
(f) The sailor helped the old lady into the lifeboat *carefully*.
(g) The nurse took the child *to America*.
(h) I'll see you *next Sunday*.
(i) I've *rarely* met him.
(j) Come up and see me *tonight*.

UNIT 4.8 PREPOSITIONAL PHRASES Form and function

TASK ONE

It was **in** the evening **on** Friday 29th March in Tribeca, New York. Police patrolman Swaine and assistant patrolman Bradley were driving **along** 3rd Avenue. Swaine stopped the patrol car, which was new and shining, **by** an electrical store. He needed some batteries. He got **out** and went **into** the store; but he left the keys **in** the car because Bradley stayed **in** the car. Swaine looked **across/down/up** the street. It was crowded **with** early evening shoppers. It was brightly lit and lively.

Suddenly, the door **by** the driver's seat opened and a young man got **into** the car. 'I gotta go,' he said. Bradley wasn't sure what was happening. As the young man tried to start the car, Bradley held **on to** the gear stick. Soon the two men were struggling **in** the front **of** the car.

Every evening Dave Merry went **for** a ride **on** his bike. He did it mainly **for** exercise, but he also enjoyed going **into** the city by bike. He liked weaving **in** and **out of** the traffic. **On** this evening, he saw the two men struggling **in** the front **of** the car. He got **off** his bike and ran **to** the car.

Meanwhile, a man **in** the corner **of** the shop saw what was happening and told patrolman Swaine. Swaine ran **out of** the shop. He saw the cyclist banging **on** the car. He thought he was the criminal. He pulled him **away from** the car. The cyclist fell **on to** the ground. He was astonished and started struggling with Swaine. Then Swaine saw the fight **in** the car. He freed himself **from** the cyclist. He got **up** and went **to** the car. He pulled open the door. Soon the criminal was overcome.

UNIT 4.9 TOO, VERY, ENOUGH Form

TASK ONE

(a) He was **too** late to go to the party.
(b) She was old **enough** to go to see the film alone.
(c) It was a **very** exciting book.
(d) There weren't **enough** chairs for everyone at the meeting.
(e) It's **very** hot at Christmas in Australia.
(f) The old lady didn't like summer in North Africa. It was **too** hot for her.
(g) London is a **very** big city.
(h) I don't like her ideas but I think she's a **very** clever politician.
(i) When the leader died, the people became **very** violent.
(j) Is it warm **enough** for you? I can put the heating on if you're cold.

UNIT 4.10 TOO, VERY, ENOUGH Function

TASK ONE

Possible answers:
(a) She's too poor to buy the car.
   He's rich enough to buy the car.
(b) It's too cold to go out.
(c) The mountain is too dangerous to climb.
(d) It's very hot in India.
(e) She has enough money to buy the book.
(f) The house on the hill is very big.

TASK TWO

Tim Merlyn is a **very** strange man. The people where he lives think he's **very** mean. He's **too** mean to give money to help the poor, although he is **very** rich. He has a house which is big **enough** for two families to live in but he never offers help to the homeless. He never goes out and is always **very** angry when someone knocks on his door.

TASK FOUR

(a) That's enough.
(b) It's all too true.

UNIT 4.11 RELATIVE CLAUSES: WHO, WHICH, THAT Form

TASK ONE

Possible answers:
(a) the man who played golf before tea
(b) the woman who always drank a lot of tea
(c) the jewels which belonged to the Queen
(d) the horse which lost the race
(e) the fox that ate the chickens
(f) the girl who loved dancing
(g) the boy who scored three goals in the football match
(h) the house which was haunted
(i) the town which was flooded by the sea
(j) the bird which sang sweetly

TASK TWO

Many years ago I went for a holiday in Aoshima, **which is a small village in Kyushu,** **which is one of the islands of Japan**. In the evening I went to a small restaurant, **which** **was in the main street running through the village**. It was a cold evening and the restaurant was empty. After a while, a man, **who was the owner**, came in. He saw me and started to talk. Later a few other men, **who were friends of his**, came in. They joined him and started to talk to me. I couldn't speak any Japanese and only the owner could speak English but that didn't stop them – especially one man **who was very tall** and **who** **seemed to be telling me his life story**. With everything he said, he pointed to himself. After a while, the owner brought out his projector and started to show us photographs **which were of people and places in the USA**. He hadn't been to the USA but he liked collecting photographs from there. When this was finished, the group took me to the fire station **which was just along the road**. The very tall man was the local fireman. The man **who walked with him** was the local policeman. I realised I was with the people **who** **administered the village**. The fireman opened the doors to the fire station and proudly showed us the beautiful fire engine **which was inside**. He wanted to give me a ride on it. He gave me a helmet **which belonged to one of his friends**. Everybody got on the fire engine and we were soon racing round the village sounding the alarm. Many people **who** **were woken by the noise** came out of their houses to see where the fire was. We all thought it was very funny.

UNIT 4.12 RELATIVE PRONOUN: OBJECT Form

TASK ONE

(a) That's the book (which) I bought last week.
(b) He's the man (who) I saw at your office.
(c) That's the car (which) they bought last year.
(d) It's a picture of the hotel (that) I stayed at on holiday.
(e) That's the ornament (which) I bought in Japan twenty years ago.
(f) That's the house (that) Jack built.
(g) It's a game (which) I like very much.
(h) He was the king (who) William of Normandy defeated in 1066.
(i) That's the film (which) I saw twenty years ago.
(j) Those are the drawings (which) a Polish student gave to me.

UNIT 4.13 RELATIVE CLAUSES: WHOSE, OF WHICH Form

TASK ONE

(a) He's the man whose father worked in a circus.
(b) That's the book the plot of which was trivial.

ANSWER KEY

(c) That's the girl whose mother is the headteacher.
(d) She's the woman whose father taught her to fly.
(e) He's the painter whose brother gave him a lot of money.
(f) He's the man whose poems are very popular.
(g) She's the speaker whose talks are very lively.
(h) He's the composer whose music is rarely played nowadays.

UNIT 4.14 RELATIVE CLAUSES Function

TASK ONE

(a) Switzerland, which has four national languages, is in the centre of Europe.
(b) The man who I met last night was very boring.
(c) Don, whose wife has been ill for two years, has decided to take her for a long holiday.
(d) That picture, which you painted in Japan, is very beautiful.
(e) I don't like the people who live at the end of the street.

TASK TWO

We decided to spend the weekend, **which was part of a long independence holiday**, in a small hotel **which was in the hills** where it would be cooler. We arrived late on Friday evening and went straight to bed. On the Saturday morning, **which was again very warm and sunny**, we went to a nearby pool, **which the hotel owner recommended**. It was surrounded by rocks and seemed to be very private. Soon after we arrived, a lot of children came. They were followed by their mothers. The children, **whose mothers were carrying large bundles of clothes**, quickly undressed and jumped into the pool. Then their mothers threw them some large bottles. The bottles contained some soapy water **which the children poured over themselves**. Then the mothers undid the bundles of clothes **which they had brought with them** and started to wash them and scrub them on the rocks nearby. From being a place for a quiet swim, the pool became a place, **which was both a bathroom and a laundry**. The children were very happy, and laughed and shouted as they washed each other. The mothers sang quietly as they washed their clothes. We sat quietly at the edge of the pool. We didn't know what to do.

UNIT 5.1 PRONOUNS Form

TASK ONE

Subject	Object	Possessive	Reflexive
I	me	**mine**	myself
you	you	**yours**	**yourself**
he	him	**his**	himself
she	her	hers	**herself**
it	it	**its**	**itself**
we	**us**	ours	ourselves
you	**you**	**yours**	**yourselves**
they	**them**	theirs	**themselves**

TASK TWO

(a) myself
(b) it; them/me/you/him/her/us/them
(c) ourselves
(d) it/them
(e) it/them
(f) yours/hers/his; yours/hers/his
(g) themselves
(h) themselves
(i) himself/you/him/her/me/us/them
(j) you/anyone/someone
(k) Anyone/Everyone/Anybody/Everybody
(l) Everyone/Everybody
(m) All/None/Half/Some/Many/Most/Both/Few/Neither/Several
(n) me
(o) no-one/nobody

TASK THREE

(a) they; it
(b) she; it
(c) yourself; you; you; you
(d) He; them; their; they; they
(e) I; it; it; them; it; me; them; they; I

UNIT 5.2 PRONOUNS Function

TASK ONE

(a) Andrew moved out of his house last month because he was getting very tired of the noise from the dogs in the house next to him/his. The dogs barked all day and night. They barked when they heard a noise and they barked when they didn't hear a noise. They were very big dogs and they made a lot of noise when they barked. Andrew tried using ear plugs at night to keep out the noise but they made his ears ache. Now Andrew is living in a flat in a building where dogs are not allowed.

(b) Steve Crone bought his first llama eight ears ago from a convent. The llama was a problem because it attacked the nuns. 'The llama was a problem child,' Steve Crone explained. 'It was raised by humans so it thinks I am a llama too.' Now the llama is the leader of Crone's herd of eight llamas. They live in the state of Maine in the United States. Steve Crone and his wife and their children live in Maine because they run a business taking people on hikes through the mountains on the llamas.

(c) Angela Rippon says that she uses a personal stereo. She doesn't wear it in the street. She is learning French so she uses it to improve her French. Angela Rippon says she listens to a tape for ten minutes every day. In the gym when she exercises on the walking machine, she plays pop music. She walks in time to the music beat. This helps her to keep going.

UNIT 5.3 SO, NEITHER/NOR Form

TASK ONE

(a) I hope so.
(b) He said so.
(c) I don't think so.
(d) I think so.
(e) I hope not.
(f) They said so.
(g) She said not.
(h) No, he doesn't.
(i) I hope not.
(j) I don't think so.

UNIT 5.4 AND, BUT Form and function

TASK ONE

(a) The children enjoyed the school **and** they went there early every day.
(b) The writer wasn't very good **but** she made a lot of money from her books.
(c) Everest was a great challenge to climbers **and** many people tried to climb it.
(d) Andy liked children **but** he and his wife didn't have any.
(e) The author of 'Danton's Death' died at 23 **but** he is very famous.
(f) It rains a lot in the northwest **but** it's a good place for a holiday.
(g) He looked ugly in the painting **but** he liked it.
(h) The mountain was very high and dangerous **but** she climbed it.
(i) Rome is a lovely city **and** it attracts many visitors.
(j) I have very little money **but** could I buy the picture over there?

UNIT 5.5 BECAUSE OF, BECAUSE Form and function

TASK ONE

(a) Because it was raining heavily, the gardener didn't come.
    The gardener didn't come because of the heavy rain.
(b) Because the book was very long, he couldn't finish it.
    Because of its length, he couldn't finish the book.
(c) Because the child was very heavy, the mother couldn't lift her.
(d) Because he didn't know the man, the farmer thought he was a thief.
(e) Because there were many complaints about her work, she lost her job.
    She lost her job because of the many complaints about her work.

TASK TWO

(a) They ate the fish because they caught it in the river.
(b) The fish was bad because the river was poisoned.
(c) The river was poisoned because a lorry had crashed and emptied poison into the river.
(d) The lorry crashed because the driver was going too fast.
(e) The driver was going fast because he was late.

UNIT 5.6 AFTER, BEFORE, WHEN, WHILE Form and function

TASK ONE

Alternative answers are possible.
(a) He was watching television **when** the accident happened.
(b) The cat left the mouse at the door **after** she had killed it.
(c) They left the car by the canal **while** they went to look for the boat.
(d) **While** he was going to London to see his girlfriend, she was going to Cambridge to see him.
(e) **Before** you buy a new radio, you should find out which is the best.
(f) He was climbing a mountain **when** he hurt his leg.
(g) The woman phoned her husband **after** she got the news.
(h) They were working in the garden **when** the storm broke.
(i) **Before** he left the house, he checked that everything was safe.
(j) You were sailing on the canal **while** I was painting the house.

TASK TWO

Answers here will depend on which conjunction you used in TASK ONE. Generally the following rules will apply.
The main event is first where you used **before**.
The main event is second where you used **after**.
The two events are happening at the same time where you used **while**.
The main event is interrupted where you used **when**.